Servants,
Misfits,
and Martyrs

Servants, Misfits, and Martyrs

SAINTS AND THEIR STORIES

JAMES C. HOWELL

UPPER
ROOM BOOKS™
NASHVILLE

Cover illustration: CELEBRATION © 1997 by John August Swanson
Serigraph 22½ x 30½ inches

Los Angeles artist John August Swanson is noted for his finely detailed, brilliantly colored paintings and original prints. His works are found in the Smithsonian Institution's National Museum of American History, London's Tate Gallery, the Vatican Museum's Collection of Modern Religious Art, and the Bibliothèque Nationale, Paris.

Represented by the Bergsma Gallery, Grand Rapids, Michigan, (616) 458-1776. John August Swanson paintings and limited-edition serigraphs are available from this gallery.

Full-color posters and cards of the cover art are available from the National Association for Hispanic Elderly. Benefits go to their programs of employment of seniors and housing for low-income seniors. Write or call: 3325 Wilshire Blvd. #800, Los Angeles, CA 90010, (213) 487-1922.

Cover design: Gore Studio, Inc.

First printing: 1999

Page 192 constitutes an extension of the copyright page.

LIBRARY OF CONGRESS CATALOGING-IN-PUBLICATION DATA

Howell, James C., 1955–
    Servants, misfits, and martyrs: saints and their stories / James C. Howell.
      p.   cm.
    Includes bibliographical references.
    ISBN 0-8358-0906-4
    1. Christian biography. I. Title.
    BR1700.2.H68   2000
    270' .092 ' 2 — dc21
    [B]   99-21609
                                              CIP

Printed in the United States of America

CONTENTS

ACKNOWLEDGMENTS

This is a book of stories, my personal favorites really. I chose them because I like them and because they have invaded my imagination and made me into somebody I wasn't before I heard them. Some of the stories are centuries old, while others are about people with whom I have shaken hands. Some are about saints officially recognized by the church, while others are about regular folks like the ones who live in my town. I want to tell you these stories and to try to reflect on why they matter, on the impact they can have on us and our world. More than half of them, I now realize, have been heard by my three wonderful children in the form of bedtime stories. My prayer is that they will treasure these stories and their heroes, that they will be shaped by them and hear God's call, and follow. Surely this is every parent's dream.

The cover of the book features a marvelous piece of folk art entitled *Celebration*. The artist John August Swanson delights in the gathering of people, especially in dance. The backdrop to his painting is the darkness of night. But the bright candles held by the people and the sparkling starlight outside color their fellowship as one of vibrant joy; their garments and the mosaic floor shimmer with warmth. Swanson endured several tragic events in his own life during the production of *Celebration*. The figures of his painting somehow surrounded him with hope and courage, helping him through his sadness to a rediscovery of love.

Originally Swanson set out to recreate the image of Pentecost. For me his painting recreates that mystical gathering of God's people, all God's saints who join in the startling beauty of the communion of the saints, their light banishing the darkness, forever drawing others into their circle. I tell stories to my children, and also to you, gentle reader, so that we too will find our place in the fellowship, for the windows and doors are open.

I think of those who opened windows and doors for me. When I was a child, my parents dragged me and my big sister to Civil War battlefields, to Monticello and Mt. Vernon, to the Liberty Bell and the Lincoln Memorial—and their patient efforts planted something significant yet long latent in me. As a college sophomore, I was a science kind of guy, with a slide rule in my pocket, scanning the course offering booklet for a history course to satisfy a requirement. By sheer luck, I chose "History of the Ancient World"—and was dazzled every semester thereafter by its teacher Richard Chowan. When he talked, you sensed you were crossing the Rubicon yourself or flinging victory laurels at Marathon or trembling at the sight of Hannibal's elephants. I was hooked on history and was blessed with other wonderful teachers of things historical: Carl Evans, Donald Jones, Mary Fraley, Jerry Faulkner, W. D. Davies, Bob Gregg. They may not remember me, but they constructed my memory of the past and my love for its heroes.

For a book like the one I am writing, in which I insanely try to talk about people from many epochs and places, I owe thanks primarily to people I have never met, authors of so many books I cherish so much that I refuse to loan them even to my dearest friends. Their names appear in the footnotes—and perhaps for a writer that may be the highest form of gratitude. I am grateful to David Steinmetz, who taught me church history at Duke in a manner that rivaled Richard Chowan, for reading part of my manuscript and making shrewd suggestions, as did Brian Daley of Notre Dame. Clint McCann of Eden Theological Seminary put me onto some good ideas. Several of my neighbors who are professors at Davidson College, Karl Plank, Sandy McKelway, Trent Foley, and Sam Maloney, were also very helpful. Frye Gaillard took the time to advise a total stranger, and I thank him.

Peter Krentz of Davidson College read the entire book and improved it in many ways. Andy Baxter, my brilliant associate pastor, contributed much to its final form, making the wise suggestion that the book needed more attention on the function of the church in shaping and forming saints—that saints not only correct the church when it has gone astray but are indebted to the church for its practices and grammar that enable them to do what they do.

Kathy Stark, the world's greatest church librarian, tracked down some books as only she can do. My secretaries, Alison Edmiston, Karen Bright, Terrie Stark, Linda Turner, and Cherry Stevens, all helped me with printing, copying, computing, and mailing. And Bob Wilson near the end rendered a special favor.

I married a lover of books. Lisa is such an encouragement to me, certainly as a writer but more so as a person, pastor, husband, and father. We are sharing our life with our three marvelous children, Sarah, Grace, and Noah, who rightly insist on a good story each night even as the fascinating stories of their lives are unfolding each day. It is to them I dedicate *Servants, Misfits, and Martyrs*.

INTRODUCTION

*In his holy flirtation with the world, God occa-
sionally drops a pocket handkerchief. These
handkerchiefs are called saints.*[1]

— FREDERICK BUECHNER

Every day, in myriad ways, we are bombarded with titillating images of celebrities. Michael Jordan, Madonna,
Bill Gates, Leonardo DiCaprio, Jewel—an ever-growing
constellation of stars parade before us, glamorizing wealth,
beauty, muscle, sex, and technology. It is as if there is a
grand trial, a great contest for truth going on—for our
souls. The witnesses waltz in and out, bearing powerful
testimony that all that glitters is in fact gold, that the day
is being won by those who are pretty and affluent, that if
it feels good it must be good, that this world with its plea-
sures is all there is.

Across the courtroom, a humble plaintiff quietly waits
a turn, hoping to portray a more compelling vision of life,
a truer manner of being, something deeper, something that
speaks to the marrow of our souls, an adventure that may
be misconstrued today but will endure past every tomorrow. As God lays out the case, dreaming of winning over
our hearts, the witnesses God calls do not look like the
celebrities at all. Poorly attired, wounded and weary, these
witnesses tell as much by the lines in their faces and the
glimmer of joy in their eyes as by their stories.

10

A CULTURE OF NARCISSISM

These witnesses we call saints. Christopher Lasch suggested that there is a profound difference between celebrities and saints. In a narcissistic, self-pleasing culture, we welcome celebrities because we lack imagination and courage. Traditional heroes make demands on us, but celebrities make no moral claim on us. Glittering stars in our culture merely feed our narcissism, our love of self, our addiction to everything society finds pleasurable. No one ever asks how our constant exposure to the rich and famous is supposed to make us good or wise or faithful. Even if we are trying to live faithful lives, our minds are always being reshaped, just a little, all the time, into the image of what surrounds us. But heroes — saints — stretch our imaginations and stand as imperatives, calling, wooing us into a higher, holier life.

I have written this book because my life has been forever reshaped by its stories. As I listen and live in this world, I find it so very easy just to slide downhill into the morass of our culture's values, buying into its hype, squandering too much of myself trying to fit in. I need saints, exemplary women and men, whose courage, faith, hope, and action inspire and reshape and encourage me, reminding me of my own calling, stretching me to be the person God intended me to be, so that I may settle for no less than some measure of sanctity in my own life.

Saints are never once-upon-a-time characters, stuck in the annals of history. They live and breathe when we retell their stories. But more than that, we Christians have this keen sense that these saints, even those who have died, are truly alive. They are with God. They seem, mysteriously enough, more alive now than they were during the life demarcated by their births and deaths —

and they were very much alive then, pulsating with the very life of God. They know that this life is not all there is. For them, the window into the future has been flung open, and they want to testify to us, stretching our imaginations and bequeathing us their courage.

So Great a Cloud

Hebrews 12:1 declares that "we are surrounded by so great a cloud of witnesses." This declaration was made at a turning point in the history of Christianity. Weariness had set in. In just their second generation of existence, many early Christians were already getting tired and a bit cynical about their life in a world that either yawned or balled up a fist when it encountered this new faith. Giving up, or just blending in, felt attractive.

To such fatigued believers came a rolled-up parchment, with a long sermon scrawled on its leaves. We know of it as the book of Hebrews. It was a ringing, timely call for faith and perseverance. Its greatest passage was the eleventh chapter, an inspiring roll call of the great saints who had embodied the faith in centuries gone by. Each name evoked a plethora of memories, stories, and even songs. Abel, Enoch, Abraham, Sarah, Jacob, Joseph, Moses, Rahab, Gideon, Samson, Daniel—the heroes of the Bible. But they were drawn out of the well of the past, not as mere nostalgia, not as "once upon a time" tales of yesteryear. What was at stake? "Therefore, since we are surrounded by so great a cloud of witnesses, let us also lay aside every weight and the sin that clings so closely, and let us run with perseverance the race that is set before us, looking to Jesus the pioneer and perfecter of our faith" (Heb. 12:1).

For that second generation of Christians, and for us,

not one of those witnesses is a mere fossil in the museum of religious memory. No, we *are* surrounded by them. They are very real. These witnesses continue to live and breathe before us. And they breathe new life and energy into us. They inspire and challenge us — and cure our cynicism.

BEYOND THE BIBLE

The Bible is full of saints. But in this book we will pay closer attention to saints throughout history, believers who, like you and me, had to take what we know from the pages of the Bible and make it somehow take on flesh in real life, in our world. Abraham, Moses, and Daniel can so easily be romanticized; they don't even have last names and are affixed in our minds in the form of sweet, pastel-colored, "pretend" figures. When it comes to raising up, inspiring, and using real people, God did not stop back in Bible times. The same God has continued to seize people, to call them, to make the word visible through them. They have last names and even addresses. We have realistic paintings and even photographs of saints. Their witness is realistic and compelling, unless we intentionally avert our gaze.

Early in his political career, Lyndon Baines Johnson was out one night with four other men carrying flashlights in a cemetery, fraudulently registering deceased voters. One of them came across a moss-covered, eroded tombstone not easily deciphered, and so he passed it by — until the leader of the expedition insisted on going back, declaring, "He has as much right to vote as anybody else in this cemetery." Perhaps for those of us who still live, the deciding votes should go to those who have died, those who have seen it all and who can bear truthful witness, those who have stood the test of time.

When we look at saints from the past, we do not see
total and utter perfection. Part of what makes saints fascinating is their humanity. In the biography of a saint, we
see some aspect of the gospel lived out with a clarity and
a freshness that reminds us how we should live. And the
very fact that a real, live human being managed to live in
an exemplary way rids us of our excuse, "Oh, I'm only
human." There are human lives that have been noble, faithful, courageous, and simply Christlike. We cannot dismiss
them by saying, "She must be a saint." What the cloud of
witnesses has done and believed and thought and felt is
attainable by you and me today.

Saints are not like great explorers, blazing trails previously untraversed. Rather, they creatively embody in a striking way something that has always been there in our faith,
something perhaps too long submerged, some aspect of the
faith that desperately needs recovery. Too easily we regard
beliefs as a group of principles or propositions we think in
our heads. But if Christianity is about anything at all, it is
about changed lives. Theology comes to life when it takes
on flesh, bones, muscle, movement, tears, smiles, reality.
And thank God theology has and does come to life. It is
precisely those real people who have said yes to God and
let their very selves be shaped and led by God who best
enable us to say yes and to be shaped and led ourselves.

WHERE WE'RE GOING

In this book we will contemplate many saints under eight
admittedly overlapping groupings. We begin with what
we'll call "misfits." Saints in so many ways are simply odd-
balls in their environments. And thank God, Francis of
Assisi and Clarence Jordan and his daughter Jan didn't

"fit in," for it is their strangeness that is compelling. In chapter 2 we will dare to watch the deeds of the saints: whom they touch and how. Servants like Teresa of Calcutta, Dorothy Day, and Millard Fuller have with great diligence, compassion, and humility loved in practical ways those whom God loves. Then in chapter 3 we will get on our knees with the masters of prayer, the most fundamental activity of all God's witnesses. We will make bold to ask Monica, Teresa of Avila, Thérèse of Lisieux, Thomas Merton, and Henri Nouwen to "teach us to pray."

Next we will attend to three ways saints articulate what they know about God, and their voices invite us to join theirs in expressing the truth. We will sit at the feet of the greatest teachers in the history of the church (chapter 4), Augustine, Martin Luther, Karl Barth, and C. S. Lewis, who have in times of deep crisis formulated doctrines and ways of thinking that are valid and trustworthy. Preachers will be heard from in chapter 5, for it is the peculiar essence of the Christian faith that everything hangs on the proclamation of the gospel; we will sit in a crowd and hear John Chrysostom, George Whitefield, Sojourner Truth, Martin Niemöller, and Billy Graham. Chapter 6 will feature singers, psalmists and poets, and hymn writers (Dante Alighieri, Charles Wesley, Isaac Watts, John Newton) whose intimacy with God has issued in beautiful lyrics of praise and adoration.

Toward the end of the book, we will explore what sadly has happened toward the end of the lives of many saints — and at the end of our Lord's life. Many believers have been so odd and have lived so faithfully that they have wound up in jail (chapter 7). Prisoners like Thomas More, Dietrich Bonhoeffer, Natan Sharansky, and Charles Colson bring a gripping perspective, especially regarding who is free and who isn't. Then in chapter 8 we will turn to martyrs, people whose devotion to God was so passionate that they actually preferred to be killed rather than feign normalcy. Polycarp, Thomas Becket, Martin Luther King, Oscar Romero, and Jean Donovan approach the bench with the ultimate witness in God's case.

As you read, I hope you will leap forward and say, "But he left out my favorite saint!" Space permits only a selection of stories, and invariably I include my personal favorites, those who sparkle in my private treasury of anecdotes. I hope you will have some of your own, some from olden times, and even better, from your own life, witnesses who move and vibrate with the very life of God for you.

AN INVITATION TO BE FRIENDS OF GOD

We will resist the temptation to allow our saints to stiffen into pretty figures in marble, relics of some bygone era. Pygmalion discovered that you cannot have a fulfilling relationship with a statue. If we listen, we can hear the saints breathing and speaking.

They do not need our whitewashing. All the saints had their foibles, their dark side, their embarrassing moments. But for us flawed mortals, even their flaws are beacons of hope, hope that God can use even us, in spite of our inadequacies. We will see that it is often the case that God uses saints precisely through their weaknesses. For us would-be saints, it is hopeful to know that our giftedness can emerge out of that place where we have been wounded.

As the saints tell us about ourselves and invite us to a truer embodiment of who we really are, they tell us even more about God. God comes to us through real people, not just off the printed page, not just in the privacy of prayer. If you would know God, become acquainted with God's friends.

The friends of God are not superhuman. Saints do not possess an extra layer of muscle. They are not taller, and they do not sport superior IQs. They are not richer, and their parents are not more clever than yours or mine. They have no batlike perception that enables them to fly in the dark. They are flesh and blood, just like you and me, no stronger, no more intelligent. And that is the point. They simply offer themselves to God, knowing they are not the elite, fully cognizant that they are inadequate to the task, that their abilities are limited and fallible.

Our cloud of witnesses features men and women, young and old, ancient and modern, tall and short. Perhaps the world has revered politicians, geniuses, and those who are agile or wealthy. But the saints are those whose mundane lives have been seized by God and used in ways to which we are wise to pay attention. God talks with us and stands before us through their witness. They are God's flirtation with us, God's wooing of our lives; a plea, an invitation to us to be friends of God and therefore—dare we say it?—saints.

CHAPTER ONE

⎡ Misfits ⎤

*It is the paradox of history that each generation
is converted by the saint who contradicts it most.*[1]

—G. K. CHESTERTON

If we look into the lives of the saints, we had best brace
ourselves for a shock. Saints are not like the rest of us, only
more so. They do not epitomize in some grand fashion all
that our culture holds dear. As Carroll Stuhlmueller suggested in *Time*, "Saints tend to be on the outer edge, where
the maniacs, the idiots and the geniuses are. They break
the mould." And Martin Marty was right when he said, "A
saint has to be a misfit. A person who embodies what his
culture considers typical or normal cannot be exemplary."
    We are trained to be suspicious of misfits, for they
threaten the status quo. But frequently it is the outsider,
the strange one, who helps us see the truth of things. In
her great story "A Good Man Is Hard to Find," Flannery
O'Connor tells about a family that has a minor car accident out in the middle of nowhere. Unfortunately, a violent man called The Misfit (who is no saint!), stumbles
upon them and terrifies them all. The grandmother pleads
for mercy and tries to tell him that if he would just pray,
Jesus would help him. "I don't want no hep," he says, "I'm
doing all right by myself."[2] Saints do want hep. They know

18

they need help, that by themselves they merely live and then die. They depend on God.

In that sense, they are the misfits—for we live in a culture where needing help is despised as a sign of weakness to be avoided at all costs. But that is where we must begin, with misfits, who are not like everybody else, who stand out in their dependence upon God. A saint is incapable of blending into the landscape and has no desire to fit in. It is the strangeness of the saint that enables her to pique our curiosity, to point the way toward what is truly precious. Jesus said Christians are to be in, not of, the world (John 17:14-18), so we need not be surprised when somebody who follows Christ lives in an odd, contradictory, and seemingly crazed manner.

A Cloud of Troublers

The Bible has its share of bizarre, contradictory characters. Noah hammered away on his ark while no one else was calling for rain (Genesis 6). At Shiloh, Hannah prayed so intently (and no one had seen such praying before) that Eli perceived her in terms utterly familiar to his culture (and to ours): She must be drunk (1 Samuel 1). The apostle Paul crazily advised the early Christians not to marry, to shirk circumcision, to miss out on business opportunities because of their commitments to Christ and the church. He landed in prison, ridiculed as either a "disturber" or a "fool" (Acts 16:20; 1 Cor. 4:10).

Shadrach, Meshach, and Abednego might have been tempted to blend in with Babylonian society, to eat and drink and worship as the Chaldeans did (Daniel 3). Nebuchadnezzar erected an astonishingly skinny, ninety-foot-tall statue of gold on the plain of Dura and expected all the residents of Babylon to bow down and worship. Three Jews, Shadrach, Meshach, and Abednego, refused — and were summarily threatened with being cast into a blazing furnace. But, in an early instance of civil disobedience, they refused to bow down. When threatened with being toasted in the fiery furnace, they made a most astonishing reply. They did not say, "God will rescue us." Rather, they said something more profound, more faithful, and even more shocking: "Our God is able to rescue us from the flames. But even if God does not, we still will not bow down and worship" (AP). Three misfits, who nevertheless are not alone in their strangeness. As children sing in Sunday school, "It's cool in the furnace!" Nebuchadnezzar peered into the flames and saw not three persons but four walking around, not even breaking a sweat. It was their oddness that led the king of Babylon to inquire about their God.

The early centuries of Christianity produced an intriguing assemblage of men and women who could be counted as "just plain weird," so zealous and strange was their embodiment of the faith. Simeon Stylites, in a feat worthy of Guinness, climbed atop a sixty-foot pillar in the year 423 and didn't come down until they hoisted down his corpse — thirty-six years later, Simeon having spent all that time in prayer. Origen, a third century theologian of unsurpassed genius, castrated himself. Vibia Perpetua, a twenty-two year old mother, deliberately courted martyrdom; in the year 203 she was gored by a bull in a Roman arena. If these misfits have lessons for us, they are subtle, far from obvious.

FRANCIS OF ASSISI

It was the Middle Ages that saw history's greatest saints. A pregnant woman dreamed she gave birth to a dog with

Dominican Order

a torch in his mouth. Her son turned out to be Saint Dominic. His was a life of humility, holiness, and service, giving birth to a band of Catholics alive and active now, eight centuries later. Legend has it that Dominic once made a pilgrimage to Rome. The pope took him on a personal tour of the gilded, opulent Lateran basilica of Saint John. Alluding to what Peter and John said to the lame man in Acts 3:6, the pope boasted, "Peter can no longer say 'Silver and gold have I none.'" But the humble Dominic answered, "No, and neither can he now say 'Rise and walk.'"[3]

Another woman, while her husband was abroad at a cloth fair, gave birth to a boy and named him Giovanni. As an adolescent, he affected a French accent and manners, and played the troubadour so exquisitely that his friends dubbed him "frenchy," or as we know him, Francis.[4]

His promising future in his father's cloth business collided with an unexpected destiny when war broke out against Perugia. Francis suited up as a knight for battle with the other young men of Assisi, but the result was disastrous. He was captured at Ponte San Giovanni in 1202 and languished, gravely ill, for months. He had visions, perhaps from his fever or perhaps from God (or both), that led him to reassess all he was about.

Francis began to pray in a crumbling old church, San Damiano, over whose altar hovered a Romanesque crucifix. One day Jesus spoke — yes, spoke — to Francis from that crucifix. "Go, rebuild my church, for as you can see, it is falling into ruin."[5] Francis heard this as a call to rebuild the stone edifice in which he knelt — and did so, with his own hands.

But the scope of that calling became evident a couple of years later when Francis went on pilgrimage to Rome. Appearing at Pope Innocent III's door in tattered clothes, he was turned away by the guard. But that night, the pope had a haunting dream: The great Lateran basilica of Saint John, the same grand church Dominic had toured, was teetering, on the verge of crashing to the earth—but was being propped up by a mysterious young man, a mere peasant. The pope recognized him as the one who had been rebuffed the previous day. Francis was found, and his new order was blessed.

When Francis was converted, he indeed initiated a new order. But it was not so much a novel organization as it was a creative way of being. Or better: an older, yet strangely familiar, way of being. Francis sought in all things to be like Jesus. G. K. Chesterton called him a mirror of Christ—in the same way the moon reflects the light of the sun. Christ, being God's son, may seem too bright, like the sun itself, too holy for us to look at long enough to see our lives in him. But Francis, like the moon, is closer to us, a mere mortal, a bearable reflection of the sun's light. Murray Bodo noticed the same thing: "It is easier to rationalize and dismiss Jesus than Francis, because Jesus, after all, is divine and so far above us. But Francis is only human like us. What he is, we can become."[6]

A Startling Naïveté

Bernard of Quintavalle, a wealthy merchant, invited Francis to his home. After the evening meal, they retired for the evening. Francis pretended to sleep; Bernard also pretended to sleep, even feigning a snore. Francis rose and then knelt, praying over and over all night long, "My God, my all." Bernard was touched and asked Francis in the morning how to become a servant of God.

The two of them went to a church called San Niccolo, where Francis asked that the Bible be opened three times.

The Catholic Workers

The resulting trio of verses is utterly familiar, yet most of us never take them seriously: "Sell your possessions, and give the money to the poor" (Matt. 19:21); "Take nothing for your journey" (Luke 9:3); and "If any want to become my followers, let them deny themselves" (Matt. 16:24). Francis, with a startling naïveté, thought he was supposed to do these things. And he did. Bernard too became poor, as did other young men, Giles, Masseo, Leo, and even women, especially Clare. So alarmed were the fathers of the city that they quarantined the young men, fearing (rightly!) that some strange sort of contagion had broken loose.

they didn't record women in history as they did men—

In 1984 I visited Assisi with a friend. We toured the city with all its sacred sites, the places where he knelt before the crucifix, where he parted ways with his father, where he cared for lepers. In the evenings, I read a copy of *The Little Flowers*, those enchanting tales from the saint's life. During our last night at the hotel, somehow I was awakened in the middle of the night and couldn't get back to sleep. For me, that night proved to be like the one Jacob spent by the river, when he wrestled all night with a stranger, perhaps an angel. Intellectually, I had learned much about Francis—but his memory shook me by the shoulders that night. In the face of his oddness, his extravagance, his utter devotion to Christ, I sensed how bland my own faith had become, how comfortably I managed to "fit in" to our culture, risking next to nothing; I was hardly a fool for Christ. I prayed for the rest of the night, as Francis had prayed near that very spot eight centuries earlier.

Since that night, I have not become the new Saint Francis. But I am at least a little more reckless, a little more passionate about God, the poor, and being holy.

Crossing All Barriers   Life is theatre—

We almost get the sense that Francis thought of himself as on stage, creating little scenes with lessons in holiness. Francis and his followers were odd, strange, noticeably different—and they transformed the face of life throughout Italy and eventually Europe and beyond. Francis surprisingly joined a horde of soldiers and knights, led by Leopold of Austria and John of Brienne, in the Fifth Crusade against Islamic Arabs in the Middle East. Late in the summer of 1219, the crusaders were arrayed in battle-ready formation at Damietta in Egypt. Francis, barefoot and with no shield or sword, walked bravely across no man's land toward the Arab army. The Muslims at first drew their sabers to kill him. But he was so pitiful, so defenseless, that they spared him, leading him to the sultan, Malik al-Kamil, who became intrigued with the faith of this misfit soldier. Were it not for the sultan's fear of his own soldiers, Francis would have pulled off the most unlikely conversion in history. He did manage to secure a little peace in a war-ravaged corner of the globe.

Sister Teresa

So holy was Francis's life that friends compared him to Jesus himself. Francis sought to imitate Christ but always with utter humility. Once he fasted forty days but on the last day ate half a loaf of bread—to be careful not to become puffed up with pride, thinking himself somehow equal to Christ. So great was his devotion to the Lord that he climbed Mount Alverno and prayed,

> My Lord Jesus Christ, I pray you to grant me two graces before I die. The first is that during my life I may feel in my soul and in my body, as much as possible, that pain that you, dear Jesus, sustained in the hour of your most bitter Passion. The second is that I may feel in my heart, as much as possible, that great love with which

you, O Son of God, were inflamed in willingly enduring
such suffering for us sinners.[7]

Wounds in his hands, feet, and side (called the *stigmata*)
appeared and bled intermittently for the balance of his life.
Throughout history there have been other "stigmatics,"
women and men who are so passionate about Jesus, so
moved by his crucifixion, that they too have mysteriously
exhibited open wounds similar to Christ's.

CLARENCE JORDAN

Stories of saints are not
all from long ago and far
away. In 1912 Mr. and
Mrs. J. W. Jordan of
Talbotton, Georgia, cel-
ebrated the birth of the
fourth of their seven
children—a boy named
Clarence.[8] Growing up
in the Baptist church, he
was one of those souls
with a natural sensitivity
to hypocrisy. After sing-
ing "Red and yellow,
black and white, they
are precious in his sight," he wondered why black children
were dressed so shabbily. He saw deacons who could
dreamily sing hymns about their love for Jesus, then turn
around and harass and even torture blacks on the rack.

In college Jordan studied agriculture, pursuing his
vision of improving the plight of poor farmers. His ROTC
commitment clashed with what he kept reading in his

Bible: How could he be a soldier and follow Jesus, who said to love your enemies? His struggle of conscience eventually led him to Southern Baptist Theological Seminary in Louisville, Kentucky, where he managed yet another degree, this one a doctorate in Greek New Testament!

Jordan became famous for his homespun translation of the New Testament, the clever and humorous Cotton Patch Version. When he translated the Good Samaritan story, he imagined that a man was robbed somewhere between Atlanta and Albany. A white preacher and a gospel song leader passed by before a black man stopped to help. The Pharisees always were cast as "Sunday school teachers."

Bible Stuff

Jordan's most brilliant translation of the New Testament did not appear in print, but in the red earth of Georgia and in the lives of people he worked, ate, and argued with. In 1942 Jordan started Koinonia Farm outside the county-seat town of Americus. He wanted blacks and whites to live together, to embody the kind of community life described in the book of Acts (2:42-45; 4:32-37), where fellowship (*koinonia* in Greek) meant communal sharing of all goods. Georgia of the forties and fifties was not exactly ready for this kind of real-life implementation of the gospel. Jordan and the Farm were ridiculed and attacked at every turn. The Ku Klux Klan repeatedly terrorized, bombed, and vandalized Koinonia.

In 1948 Jordan brought a dark-skinned man (actually an Indian) to the local Baptist church. The deacons demanded Jordan meet with them, and they asked that he desist from this kind of troublemaking. He handed one of them a Bible, requesting that the deacons show him where it says in the Book that a dark-skinned man shouldn't enter the house of the Lord. "Brethren, if I have violated any teaching of this book in my beliefs or conduct, I will withdraw quietly from this church fellowship. Please point to the text or teaching I have failed to try to live up to!" The deacon silently handed the Bible to another, who handed it to yet another, who slammed the Book on the table and shouted, "Don't give me that scripture stuff!" Jordan got the last word: "No, I'm asking you to give it to me."[9] That day Jordan and his friends became "ex-Baptists."

Jordan's saucy yet hauntingly true remarks are legendary. A Klan delegation visited Koinonia and announced to Jordan, "We don't allow the sun to set on any white man who eats with a nigger." He smiled and replied, "I'm a Baptist preacher, and I've heard of men with power over the sun. But until today I never hoped to meet one."[10]

After preaching at a gilded, cathedral-like church in Atlanta, Jordan was asked for some advice by the pastor. Their custodian had eight children and worked seven days a week for a mere eighty dollars per week. The concerned minister claimed he tried to get the man a raise but with no success. Jordan considered this for a minute and then said, "Why not just swap salaries with the janitor? That wouldn't require any extra money in the budget."[11]

To another pastor, who proudly pointed to the fancy new ten-thousand dollar cross adorning his sanctuary, Jordan responded that at one time Christians could get those crosses for free. Jordan's preaching featured splendid phrasings: "God is not 'in his heaven with all well on the earth.' He is on this earth, and all hell's broke loose." Or "The good news of the resurrection is not that we shall die and go home with him, but that he has risen and comes home with us, bringing all his hungry, naked, thirsty, sick, prisoner brothers with him."[12]

Do You Have a Church?

After one of many visits from KKK intimidators, Jordan said, "It was not a question of whether or not we were to be scared,...but whether or not we would be *obedient*."[13] Koinonia perched itself on the American landscape as a call to obedience—and the church responded poorly.

Jordan once asked his brother, Robert (who became a state senator and a justice on the state Supreme Court), to be Koinonia's attorney. "I can't do that. You know my political aspirations. I might lose my job, my house, everything I've got."

Clarence said, "*We* might lose everything too."

"It's different for you," Robert responded.

"Why is it different?...You and I joined the church the same Sunday as boys. I expect when we came forward the preacher asked,...'Do you accept Jesus as your Lord and Savior?' And I said, 'Yes.' What did you say?"

Robert replied, "I follow Jesus, Clarence, up to a point."

"Could that point by any chance be—the cross?"

"I follow him to the cross, but not *on* the cross. I'm not getting myself crucified."

"Then I don't believe you are a disciple. You're an admirer of Jesus, but not a disciple of his. I think you ought to go back to the church you belong to, and tell them you're an admirer not a disciple."

"Well now, if everyone who felt like I do did that, we wouldn't *have* a church, would we?" To which Clarence applied the coup de grace: "The question is, Do you have a church?"[14] Later Robert saw the light, became a disciple himself, and boasted that his brother was the greatest Christian he had ever known.

Fifteen Minutes

Clarence's daughter Jan was hassled and ostracized at school. One especially vicious boy, Bob Speck, called her names and threw her books down repeatedly. After a few weeks, Clarence decided he had heard enough of this harassment and told his daughter, "I'm going to come to school this afternoon.... I've tried to be a follower of Jesus, and he taught me to love my enemies and all like that, but at that time I'm going to ask Jesus to excuse me for about fifteen minutes while I beat the hell out of Bob Speck."

Jan said, "Daddy, you can't be excused from being a Christian for fifteen minutes." So Clarence suggested: "I want you to let your fingernails grow about three inches. And when Bob Speck calls you those names, I want you to throw the whole bunch of books in his face and jump on him and scratch his eyes out, because I think for a kid to be scratched up by a girl would be a good lesson for him." Again she said, "You're not serious."

Two weeks passed, and Clarence had not heard a word about Bob Speck. When he asked Jan about it, she reported, "He doesn't bother me any more."

Dad was stunned: "Has he moved?"

"No, he's still there."

"Oh, has he been converted?"

"No," she answered.

"Does he call you any names?"

"No, never."

"Well what happened?"

Jan told her story: "Well, I got to figuring that I'm a little taller than Bob and I could see him coming before he could see me. When I'd see him, I'd begin smiling and waving and gushing at him like I was just head over heels in love with him…like I was going to eat him up. The other kids got to teasing him about me having a crush on him, and now, the only time I see him is when he peeps around the corner to see if I'm coming. If I am, he goes all the way round the outside."[15]

Clarence Jordan died suddenly and prematurely of heart failure on October 29, 1969, a mere fifty-seven years old. He was buried wearing old blue jeans out in the field at Koinonia, not far from the shack he called his office. Some time later, his wife Florence was asked the whereabouts of his grave. "We planted him out there somewhere."

ON BEING A MISFIT

Jordan was a saint, one of that great cloud of witnesses we call misfits. Misfits can point a bright light on the ways we are out of sync with God: Do you have a church? If you follow Jesus, is there some point where you shrink back? Where is the hypocrisy in your life? For how many minutes do you forsake your Christianity? Have you ever thought about swapping salaries with anyone?

These are not random questions. They grow right out of the scriptures. Saints read the Bible with a startling naïveté—and they think they are supposed to go and do it. Francis, Dominic, and Clarence Jordan all took the Bible "literally," not in the sense of defending the accuracy of this or that detail but in the more provocative sense of taking it personally, assuming it means what it says. God gave us the Bible, not just to wave it about and certainly not for it to collect dust on a coffee table, but so it could guide our lives. The Bible is an invitation to us to come home, to be the people we were made to be, to do what we were made to do.

Therefore, misfits aren't misfits at all. Holiness only appears to be abnormal. The truth is, holiness is normal; to be anything else is to be abnormal. Being a saint is simply being the person God made me to be. Saints at the end of the day are not really strange or odd or misfits. They are simply real, or normal. They actually are what we all are made to be, what we can be.

WHERE THE BATTLE RAGES

To qualify as a saintly misfit, we cannot be just plain strange. Being different in itself may be nothing but quirkiness, not saintliness. Rather, saints differ from the culture 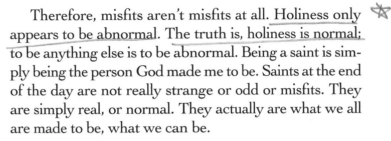 in the same way that Jesus differed from his culture. Jordan told about a church in Georgia that installed a fabulous fountain on its lawn while neighbors had no running water: "As long as God is God and not man, we know how to handle him—we can build him a fountain on the lawn. But as soon as we see God as man, then we have to give him a cup of water."[16]

We need to contemplate saints, especially as they expose points of conflict between the culture and the gospel. In a letter, Martin Luther once wrote, "If I profess with the loudest voice and clearest exposition every portion of the truth of God except precisely that little point at which the world and the devil are at that moment attacking, I am not *confessing* Christ. Where the battle rages, there the loyalty of the soldier is proved."[17]

In our world, those little points are many. But perhaps the battle rages most furiously nowadays on the green fields of wealth. Our society has a bloated attachment to money and all it signifies. The witness of Francis, who was rich, yet intentionally became poor and a saint, begs for a verdict. Murray Bodo referred to Francis's poverty as

> a divine antidote to the disease which would infect soci-
> ety and, more importantly, the individual, from then on.
> One's personal value and self-esteem would by and
> large be measured in proportion to an ability to make
> money. ...Money and what it represents becomes the
> fullness of life....[Francis] was the quintessential
> Christian who saw what money would do to the spirit.
> Christ alone is the fullness of life, and the compulsive
> pursuit of money, more than anything else, distracts the
> individual from what really brings life.[18]

THE SALT OF THE EARTH

But misfits never just pass judgment. Rather, through their
oddness they lovingly engage and wrap their arms around
all that is out of sync with God. "You are the salt of the
earth" (Matt. 5:13) — and salt flavors and preserves. G. K.
Chesterton offered a lovely thought on our role as salt:
"Salt seasons and preserves beef, not because it is like beef;
but because it is very unlike it. Christ did not tell his apostles that they were only the excellent people, or the only
excellent people, but that they were the exceptional people; the permanently incongruous and incompatible people; and the text about the salt of the earth is really as sharp
and shrewd and tart as the taste of salt."[19] Francis and
Clarence Jordan were exceptional and incongruous — and
always full of love. What they did, you and I can do.

On the night of October 3, 1226, Francis died. His last
words were, "I have done what is mine to do; may Christ
teach you what is yours to do."[20] This invitation was reit-
erated not long ago by Henri Nouwen, who pressed a crucial question for me and for you: "Who will be the St.
Francis of our age?"[21]

CHAPTER TWO

SERVANTS

We don't have to be heroes.... We don't have to do big things, but to live each day in love, doing little things, learning to welcome one another, particularly the weak and those in pain.[1]

—JEAN VANIER

There have actually been many Saint Francises in our day and in every age. Their saltiness, their incongruity takes many forms, but none perhaps as compelling as that of the servant. Jesus humbly served people who were lonely, afraid, sick, weary—and it is this humble, meek, selfless, tender Christ that is not seen often enough in our day. But when he becomes visible in the person of real servants of faith, lives are changed. Most servants, because of their humility, remain shrouded in the anonymity of good deeds. But others have registered their heroic exploits in the annals of history, and their witness is compelling.

An atheist watched one such servant as she went about her business. Later he claimed that he had seen Jesus for the first time in his life—and in Calcutta of all places. Mother Teresa, short of stature, stood tall in the public eye.[2] She was a misfit to be sure. Those intriguing photos of Mother Teresa with the beautiful Princess Diana unveil the stark contrast between a short, wrinkled servant of the

Mother Teresa and Princess Diana

AP / Wide World Photo

poor, clad in a simple sari, and the Western ideal of womanhood, chic and stylish, generous in a glitzy and convenient sort of way. Mother Teresa never followed the crowd. Or we should say she gave herself to someone in the crowd no one else noticed, one poor person at a time.

TERESA OF CALCUTTA

Born on August 27, 1910, she was named Agnes by her affluent and devout Albanian parents, Nikola and Dranafile Bojaxhiu. By her teenage years she had an insatiable craving to live and serve in India. She joined the Sisters of Loreto and took the name Teresa, after Thérèse of Lisieux, about whom we will learn more in the next chapter. She became a teacher to affluent Bengali girls in Calcutta, though rules of enclosure kept her closeted from the real life of the city. But in 1946, on the train to Darjeeling, she heard a voice calling her to reach out to the poorest of the poor. She left the security of her school to live among the destitute of Calcutta.

At first Teresa had no helper, no money, no shelter, no security. With a small bag she walked into the slums, unsure where to go. Like the poor, she had to search on foot for a roof over her head. She began to understand the exhaustion of the poor, the scarcity of food, the inaccessibility of medicine. She rented a little hut for five rupees a month and invited children to her makeshift school. Beyond teaching, much of her time was spent in the work of bathing, carrying, and feeding.

Engaging Others

One morning, she prepared a list of medicines and appealed to a pharmacist. He claimed he could not possibly help. She simply sat down and prayed, just outside his office all day—at the end of which he gave her all she needed. Throughout her life she exhibited this dogged persistence that not only secured what the poor needed, but she engaged others who had previously been hesitant to serve. Her mission was to find food and medicine, but mostly it was to love. Thousands, quite literally, could be counted as "failures": They died while she was with them. But her mission was to love, to lend to strangers the greatest of all dignities, that one need not die alone.

One by one she picked up thousands of the destitute and suffering. One by one she took other young women by the hand and set them to picking up the destitute and suffering. Girls she had taught began to follow her into the streets—and for many the work meant descending many notches in the Indian caste system. Once a wealthy Hindu woman came, offering aid. During the conversation, she admitted how much she loved beautiful saris; in fact, she spent eight hundred rupees each month on a new sari. Mother Teresa, whose distinctive white cotton sari with a blue stripe cost eight rupees, thought this the place to begin. "Next time, when you go to buy a sari, instead of buying a sari for eight hundred rupees, you buy a sari worth five hundred rupees and with the remaining three hundred you buy saris for the poor people."[3] More than the shifting of money was at stake; the elegance of a sari was a symbol of a woman's status, her notch in the caste system. But the woman did it and over time came down to paying just one hundred rupees for her sari, giving the rest away. Teresa urged her, "Please do not go below one hundred!" The woman reported that her life was transformed, that she received far more than she ever gave.

We Are Doing It to Jesus

Everything hinged on Mother Teresa's sense of the presence of Christ in the poor. In many ways, her life was an embodied sermon on Matthew 25:31-46, Jesus' last lesson that was for her both a blueprint for action and a source of joy. "The Missionaries of Charity do firmly believe that they are touching the body of Christ in his distressing disguise whenever they are helping and touching the poor. We cannot do this with a long face."[4] For Mother Teresa service was not somehow the outcome of prayer or something done when not praying. Serving the poor and opening the heart to Christ were one and the same. She taught the sisters "to pray while working, doing it for Jesus and doing it to Jesus. This brings a tremendous closeness with him."[5]

Mother Teresa spoke on this theme all over the world and with a pointed urgency.

> At the end of life we will not be judged by
> how many diplomas we have received
> how much money we have made
> how many great things we have done.
>
> We will be judged by
> "I was hungry and you gave me to eat
> I was naked and you clothed me
> I was homeless and you took me in."[6]

While her focus was never on "how many," the growth of her ministry was unparalleled. In 1948 she was an army of one. By 1950 she had seven sisters, by 1960 she had 119, by 1970 she had 585, and by her death in 1997 over a thousand. By 1980 she had started 140 schools in the slums, housed 4,000 children in 70 homes, arranged over 1,000 adoptions per year, operated 81 homes for the dying and 670 mobile clinics treating millions, and fed 50,000 a day at 300 meal sites.

A Sign from God

Teresa's fame was itself remarkable. Cynics suggested that she sought and basked in the light of media coverage. Other critics said people supported and admired her to assuage their own self-indulgent guilt. But perhaps Teresa was for the twentieth century a sign from God, a beacon of hope, at least one person who positively and beautifully reminded us of what the presence of Christ looks like in the flesh. She certainly handled all the publicity with considerable aplomb. In 1964 Pope Paul VI gave her a white Cadillac. She in turn raffled it off for 460,000 rupees ($100,000 in U.S. currency) and invested the money in her new home for the poor in Venezuela. When she was awarded the Nobel Peace Prize in 1979, she refused the customary banquet, directing that the budgeted £3,000 be given to the poor enduring an inordinately harsh winter in Oslo.

Two years before Mother Teresa died, I took my seven-year-old daughter to see her in the Charlotte Coliseum. When Mother Teresa walked on stage and the tumultuous applause finally died down, my daughter said, "Daddy, she looks like somebody in the Bible." Indeed she did.

SERVANTS THROUGH HISTORY

The history of the Christian church has had its share of exemplary servants. In the eleventh century Margaret became queen of Scotland, marrying Malcolm, who had succeeded Macbeth (whom Shakespeare made famous). So noteworthy was her goodness that no one would do or say anything unkind or unholy in her presence. Great throngs of the poor crowded into the palace each day, where Margaret and Malcolm fed them personally. She always took plenty of cash when she went on a journey and distributed it to the poor at her destination. Many orphans and destitute families lived entirely at her expense.

Thomas Becket, born in London in 1118, will be one of the martyrs we will reflect upon in the last chapter. While he was archbishop of Canterbury, the most august ecclesiastical position in the entire realm of England, he ate only simple, modest meals, taking great care to feed the poor around Canterbury. Each morning he personally fed and washed the feet of impoverished peasants—and they grieved his assassination deeply.

More recently Katharine Drexel, heiress to a hefty fortune, gave away more than $20 million before her death in 1955, most of it to educate and care for blacks and Native Americans. This Philadelphia debutante took a vow of poverty, and her stunning generosity was cloaked behind anonymity. When Xavier University, established through her funding, was dedicated, she sat in the back and refused to allow her name to be mentioned in any way.

FRANCIS OF ASSISI

In the last chapter we began to look at Francis of Assisi. Profoundly devoted to prayer, he believed that the soul devoted to God will not look like a nicely upholstered oratory, but more like a carpenter shop. Francis knew how to love. G.K. Chesterton wrote that Francis "seems to have liked everybody, but especially those whom everybody disliked him for liking." And again, "Francis had all his life a great liking for people who had been put hopelessly in the wrong."[7]

Lepers came to him. No physician would touch them—but Francis treated his "brothers in Christ" with tenderness, treating their wounds, embracing and kissing those who had been ostracized from society, even building a hospital for them. One leper was especially rude and impatient, wearing down the goodwill of even the most loving friars, who were about to throw him out. But Francis intervened and tended to the man himself. He drew a warm bath for him, sprinkled it with special herbs, and prayed intently, taking care of the man for weeks thereafter. A double miracle occurred: The man was healed not only of his leprosy but also of his nagging.

Francis was a dinner guest with many knights and nobles at the residence of the bishop of Ostia, who later became Pope Gregory IX. Not long after the meal began, Francis sneaked out to beg alms. He returned and showed them the shameful crusts he had collected and then offered them to the bishop's dinner guests as gifts of the Lord God.

Francis's love for the poor was tender, generous. His second biographer, Thomas of Celano, said "he looked upon the greatest crowd as on a single man, and with every man he would speak with as much care and attention as though he had a great multitude before him."[8] If Francis met someone on the road carrying a load, he would insist on bearing it on his own shoulders. He repeatedly took off his meager garments and gave them to the poor. Like Mother Teresa centuries later, Francis saw Christ in the faces of the poor and loved them, loving Christ.

The band of friars who joined in the crusade of Francis were remarkable in many ways. A young woman named Clare took up the mantle, let her beautiful hair be shorn, and became the epitome of holiness and charity, founding the resilient order of the Poor Clares. Within a couple of centuries, Franciscans had fanned out to serve the poor all over the world.

SOLIDARITY WITH THOSE IN NEED

We begin to see some common themes in the stories of servants. First of all, if you are going to serve, you have to give up something precious. Teresa of Calcutta forsook a comfortable life. Francis gave away his wealth; friends and family jeered, thought him a fool or a madman, threw dirt and rocks. His father, Pietro, locked him in a dungeon, and sued him in the Palazzo Communale. With great theatricality Francis stripped off his clothing, handed it all back to his father, and proclaimed, "Up to now I have called Pietro Bernardone my father, but as I am now resolved to serve God...I will say 'Our Father who art in Heaven' instead of my father 'Pietro Bernardone.'"[9] He donned the coarse garment of the simplest peasant and forsook his stylish belts for a simple rope about his waist.

His garments demonstrate how, second, service requires genuine solidarity with those in need. Francis did not toss down gold from behind Assisi's city walls. Rather, he purchased a plot of land outside the walls from a pig farmer named Gorzio, rebuilt the small church Santa Maria di Portiuncula ("the little portion"), and lived among the poor. Mother Teresa took nothing with her into the slums of Calcutta. Even into old age, when she was an international celebrity, she always took her fair turn at scrubbing the toilets. The room where she lived was modest, said to be the worst in the house, noisy and very hot.

Third and consistently throughout history, when saints look at the poor, at persons who are hurting, they see not just that person but Christ himself. Sometimes Christ can be seen most clearly in the unlikeliest of people. In 1964 a tall thirty-six-year-old Canadian with a contagious smile purchased a stone house in the village of Trosly-Breuil, just north of Paris, and invited three mentally handicapped men to live with him. Why? "Because Jesus wanted it."

JEAN VANIER

Jean Vanier was born on September 10, 1928; his father was Governor-General of Canada. After spending much of his childhood in London, he entered the navy during World War II, becoming an officer on Canada's only aircraft carrier. But he performed poorly on night-watch, preferring his prayer book to scanning the skies for enemy planes. His mother introduced him to a priest, Thomas Philippe, who in turn was acquainted with a Dr. Preuat, who thought his mentally handicapped patients would benefit from some living arrangement including a workshop. While Thomas was refurbishing a chapel to help with Dr. Preuat's work, he gently suggested to Vanier that there was "something special to be done among handicapped people."

This was God's call to Vanier. He purchased a house and invited Raphael, Philippe, and Dany to live with him. With no lavatory and no electricity, the going was rough. Dany proved too difficult to handle—and Vanier has always had a keen sense that servants are not superhuman, that they cannot surmount any and every hurdle. He named his new ministry "l'Arche," the French word for "ark" but also for "arch." "So it's the whole vision of a boat where we welcome people who are in pain. It's the place where we are saved. It's the place of the covenant....Then there is the whole idea of the arch as a bridge, the bridge between two worlds."[10]

Vanier liked the very sound of the word and reminded everyone that it was not pronounced with a hard *k* but with a soft *sh*, intimating a gentle, inviting community. There are now about a hundred l'Arche communities around the world. In Trosly-Breuil alone, four hundred residents live in twenty houses.

On the surface of things, Jean Vanier was taking care of these men, cooking, feeding, cleaning, and bathing. But he insisted that he was creating a genuine community where all give, all receive. Vanier taught us how to see Jesus in those who are broken, in those who are weak, in those who are rejected. We also get a sobering glimpse of our own fragility, our own anguish, our own eagerness to belong. "The basic gift of a handicapped person is that of having kept the heart of a child."[11] These people, regarded as useless by society, are wellsprings of great joy and fellowship. Vanier thought of his companions and marveled at "the gift God has given us in having brought us together from a place of loneliness into a sense of belonging. I know that you have accepted me and I you. I know your gifts, and I also know your darkness."[12]

In the twentieth century, no one comprehended this sharing of gifts better than a remarkable woman, to whom we now turn, who suggested that "those who cannot see Christ in the poor are atheists indeed."[13]

DOROTHY DAY

In 1983 a group of priests in Chicago initiated the rigorous process to have Dorothy Day canonized, that is, made an official "saint," fully recognized by the Roman Catholic Church. But some of Day's followers know how time-consuming and expensive the investigation into sainthood

can be. They would prefer the money and energy be given to the poor—as Day herself would have it. She actually was devoted to the saints, and she believed we are all called to be saints. Her personal history was checkered: an abortion, a divorce, a child born out of wedlock. But few people have more keenly sensed how the Christian story is lived out in the real world.

Dorothy was born November 8, 1897, in Brooklyn.[14] Reared in a fairly pious Episcopal home, she abandoned religion during her adolescent and early adult years. She frequented a saloon called the Golden Swan, befriending other Greenwich Village intellectuals like Eugene O'Neill, John Dos Passos, and Malcolm Cowley. She became enamored with the writings of Jack London (especially *Martin Eden*) and Sinclair Lewis (*The Jungle*), as she began to wake up to the plight of the poor.

In church she saw people fawning over the rich but none taking off coats to clothe the poor or having a banquet and inviting the poor, lame, and blind. This cognitive dissonance could have driven her permanently from the church. But having a daughter drove her back into the church—this time the Catholic church. She worried that she might be a traitor to the poor by entering the church, but in she came. She went to Mass. She read her Bible—and for forty-seven years never tired of doing all one person could do to make that Christian vision a reality, calling the church, to which she was something of an outsider, back to its true vocation.

The Catholic Worker

Dorothy wanted the public to know the church had a social program. Using her literary skills, she published a newspaper out of the kitchen of her tenement on East 15th Street. She sold *The Catholic Worker* for a penny a copy, cheap enough for anyone to buy and read. It challenged the laziness of an uninvolved church that ignored Christ's mandate to care for the poor. It questioned how the church could bless the powers that be, instead of lifting up the powerless. It tackled poverty, racism, and unfairness in the workplace.

The church did not always appreciate being told the truth about its calling. The very first issue of *The Catholic Worker* carried these words from Peter Maurin, Dorothy's partner in the paper:

> Christ drove the money changers
> out of the Temple.
> But today nobody dares
> to drive the money lenders out of the Temple.
> And nobody dares
> to drive the money lenders
> out of the Temple
> because the money lenders have taken a mortgage
> on the Temple.[15]

Circulation skyrocketed: 2,500 of the first issue were sold, and in three years 150,000 had to be printed.

Soon Dorothy discovered that she would have to back up her talk with action. And she did. Dorothy spent half her life publishing and the other half being a doer of her own words. She personally opened dozens of shelters with plenty of coffee and mulligan stew, places where the poor could come to eat, to pray, to make friends, and to get vocational training. The first shelter was in Dorothy's own tiny East 15th Street apartment, which also housed the paper! Lines formed outside her home, and she fed hundreds each day. No one preached at them. They were simply loved and welcomed. She filled soup bowls, cleaned the house, changed bedpans. She served.

Dorothy was exceptional in that she cared for the poor directly but also stepped back and worked for broader societal changes. As reported in the *New York Times Magazine* she never forgot the questions she harbored as a precocious child: "Whatever I had read as a child about the saints had thrilled me. I could see the nobility of giving one's life for the sick, the maimed, the leper. But why was so much done in remedying the evil instead of avoiding it in the first place?...Where were the saints to try to change the social order, not just to minister to the slaves, but to do away with slavery?"

Dorothy's service cost her dearly. She did a couple of jail stints for marching with the "Wobblies" (the Industrial Workers of the World), the vanguard of the twentieth-century labor movement. She rode freedom buses in the south during the civil rights movement. She stood with Cesar Chavez and the migrant workers in California, for she could not bear those disparities between rich and poor, favoritism and injustice.

To Have Had Him on My Mind

Dorothy Day embodied what the Bible urges on us all, that we be doers, not just hearers, of God's word (James 1:22). Her life was a visible prayer. She once said, "Does

God have a set way of prayer, a way that He expects each of us to follow? I doubt it. I believe some people—lots of people—pray through the witness of their lives, through the work they do, the friendships they have, the love they offer people and receive from people. Since when are *words* the only acceptable form of prayer?"[16]

The simplicity of her life and conversation were striking. Not long before her death in 1980, she said, "Let's all try to be poorer. My mother used to say, 'Everyone take less, and there will be room for one more.' There was always room for one more at our table."[17]

In many ways, Dorothy's own life was marked by episodes of unhappiness—but like many saints, she made great use of her own disappointments. Precisely through her own disappointments and her passion to be with others in theirs, she came to have peace, a fundamental joy, deeper and more enduring than any mere personal pleasantries. Her energy emanated from her devotional life and from an unshakable sense of being in sync with her divine calling. Shortly before her death, she shared the most remarkable thought with Robert Coles:

> I try to remember this life that the Lord gave me; the other day I wrote down the words 'a life remembered,' and I was going to try to make a summary for myself, write what mattered most—but I couldn't do it. I just sat there and thought of our Lord, and His visit to us all those centuries ago, and I said to myself that my great luck was to have had Him on my mind for so long in my life![18]

Interestingly, she once visited Clarence Jordan in Americus. During her visit, she insisted on taking her turn pulling all-night sentry duty in a station wagon at the oak tree entrance to Koinonia Farm. Since it was the night before

Easter, she passed the hours thinking of Christ's suffering. A car approached and slowed down. Just as Dorothy ducked down, bullet fire ripped into the car. Hers was not the only narrow escape from disaster at Koinonia.

MILLARD FULLER

In November of 1965, Linda Fuller told her husband Millard she was leaving him.[19] So absorbed was he in his business, in making the then unheard-of sum of a million dollars a year (even if he had to skirt his principles just a little), that he had not noticed she was slipping away. Panicked by her wake-up call, he piled her and their children into their Lincoln Continental and set off for Florida. On the way they met up with some friends in Albany, Georgia, who had moved to Clarence Jordan's Koinonia community. Millard Fuller agreed to have lunch with Jordan and wound up staying a month.

Fuller told Jordan he felt this tremendous heaviness on his chest. Wryly, Jordan suggested that "a million dollars can weigh awfully burdensome on a man." He suggested that Fuller was a "money-ac," that he was addicted to money. Jordan was successful with this young millionaire in a way Jesus wasn't with the rich young ruler, illustrating one of Jordan's great sayings: "What the poor need is not charity but capital, not caseworkers but coworkers. And what the rich need is a wise, honorable, and just way of divesting themselves of their overabundance."[20]

After Jordan's death Fuller went into the shack at Koinonia and studied the Bible. He took the Bible seriously in its condemnation of loaning at interest. He contemplated how Jordan had wanted to develop a "fund for humanity," to be able to purchase plenty of land to set up the poor on self-sustaining farms, and to provide decent housing for the poor. Fuller caught the vision and applied his genius for business — and the rest is history. At first he revitalized a tiring Koinonia Farm into Koinonia Partners, which today has a food-processing industry, a child development center, legal aid, a prison ministry, and foster child care. Most famously he founded the astonishing ministry called Habitat for Humanity, which has engaged thousands of volunteers in building nearly 100,000 quality homes for the working poor throughout America and in such far-flung locations as Zaire, Guatemala, Uganda, Ireland, and Hungary.

The Answer to My Prayer

In *Yours Are the Hands of Christ*, I told the story of Melissa Cornett, who introduced Fuller to a large crowd in Charlotte, North Carolina, by telling him, "You are the answer to my prayer. I grew up in a tenement, a terrible place, full of drugs, violence. I was nobody, knew I'd always be nobody. I had a little boy — and there he was, in a terrible place, full of drugs, violence. I knew he'd never be anybody either. So I got on my knees and I prayed. I prayed hard. I said, 'Lord, I will do anything; I will give up my life. But please, please, I just want my boy to have a chance to be somebody.' Millard Fuller, when God told you to give away your money, you were the answer to my prayer. I heard about Habitat, and I got to build a house. I met President Jimmy Carter. We got a house, a nice house. Before we moved in, my boy had started school, but his teacher said he was slow and he would probably never catch up. He never smiled. But then we moved into our new house. He had his own room. And he began to shine that day. He got to where he played and had fun.

And he started making good grades in school. Now he's in the third grade, and he's making straight A's. The other day, my boy said to me, 'Momma, do you know what I want to be when I grow up?' I said, 'No, what do you want to be?' He said, 'I'm going to be a doctor.' Millard Fuller, you're the answer to my prayer."

LESSONS OF SERVANTHOOD

Earlier we noted how saints give up something for the poor, how they actually live among the poor, how they see Christ in the poor. Servants bear witness to the tangibility of the life of faith. Dorothy Day longed for a synthesis of body and soul, of heaven and earth, the sort of thing Martin Luther King Jr. spoke of when he said, "It's alright to talk about 'long white robes over yonder,' in all of its symbolism. But ultimately people want some suits and dresses and shoes to wear down here."[21] Servants pray, "Thy will be done on earth as it is in heaven," and then work to make "over yonder" reality "down here."

Service is never just loving humanity, caring about the masses. Service proceeds slowly, one person at a time. G. K. Chesterton said that Saint Francis could not see the forest for the trees—and that he didn't want to. Clarence Jordan had a long lunch with a lawyer from Alabama, who one day built one house for a woman whose son may become a doctor. Once Mother Teresa was invited to a hunger conference in Bombay. Arriving late she found a man starving on the steps outside the building where, on the inside, they were discussing trends and food supplies and projections and budgets. Instead of going in, she picked up the man and fed him.

When you are odd in this way, you are criticized. Not

surprisingly, Mother Teresa drew criticism for never addressing the root, systemic causes of poverty. But she wasn't opposed to others addressing such big issues. Her calling was simply to care for persons who were hungry, today, one at a time.

No one is too low, and no one is too high to be involved. Millard Fuller pushed his neighbor and former President Jimmy Carter to help with Habitat for Humanity. Carter showed up one day in what seemed to be a photo-opportunity, a mere gesture of support. But Carter labored all day long, framing the home of Willie Solomon and his family. Not long afterward Carter and his wife Rosalynn pulled together work teams that renovated tenements in Manhattan. The President said it himself: "It's like eating peanuts—if we can decide to be adventurous and generous once, it may be hard to stop!"[22]

SHARING TOGETHER

Service ultimately is about community. Often, even when we are engaged in charity, there is no real community. The poor remain segregated from the warmhearted rich, who dole out some goodness and return to their comfortable lives. Jürgen Moltmann once said that the opposite of poverty is not property, but the opposite of both poverty and property is community. Service can bring rich and poor together in community, for which both are desperately hungry. Dorothy Day knew plenty of sorrow, even in a crowded city, surrounded by many people. She could never be free of this "long loneliness" without community. She wrote, "The only answer in this life, to the loneliness we are all bound to feel, is community. The living together, working together, sharing together, loving God and loving our brother, and living close to him in community so we can show our love for Him."[23]

For community to happen, we must recognize the dignity of the poor. One day a well-dressed woman visited Dorothy Day and donated a diamond ring. Dorothy thanked her and later in the day gave the ring to an elderly woman who took most of her meals at the shelter. A coworker protested, suggesting Dorothy should have sold the ring and used the money to pay the woman's rent for a year. But Dorothy insisted that the woman have her dignity. The woman could choose what to do with the ring. She could pay her rent for a year; or she could just wear the ring, like the woman who donated it. "Do you suppose that God created diamonds only for the rich?"[24]

Saints indeed point beyond themselves to the importance of all people and of God. In a *Time* magazine article, Methodist missionary Fred Morris described Dom Helder Câmara, the archbishop of Recife and noted advocate for the poor: "Being with him, watching him, listening to him, one is less and less aware of him and increasingly aware of the reality to which he points—a God who cares about the little people of the earth."

With community comes peace and joy. Who was not transfixed by the peaceful visage of Mother Teresa? Millard Fuller's marriage was healed. But we must be careful; there is a paradox here. Francis, Teresa, Day, and Fuller did not serve so they could feel good about themselves. They were not first of all seeking self-fulfillment, with service as a means to that end. Rather, they loved God, and their service grew naturally out of the soil of their faith in God.

STRONG FAITH IN GOD

What is most noteworthy about the saints is how prayer and service are not disjointed or haphazardly linked, as if they could somehow be pulled apart, one or the other standing alone. When we look at the service and the prayers of the saints, it is like looking at a sphere, something of depth, not with two sides but a cohesive thing of beauty. Mother Teresa's Missionaries of Charity follow her daily regimen of rising at 4:40 AM, prayers at 5:00, Mass at 5:45, breakfast, then work among the poor from 8 until 12:30, lunch, rest, reading and meditation at 2:30, the adoration of the blessed Sacrament from 3:15–4:30, and three more hours of service to the poor before evening prayers at 9:00.

The friends of Francis stood in awe of his intimate, joyful, and astonishingly personal relationship to God. Jim Forest said that Dorothy Day's "ability to survive community life and even to see good in those of us who came to help was surely due to the depth and intensity of her spiritual life. It was obvious to anyone who was in sight of Dorothy for more than a few hours that she was a woman of prayer. When I think of her, I recall her first of all on her knees."[25] As Dorothy said, "We feed the hungry, yes. We try to shelter the homeless and give them clothes, but there is strong faith at work; we pray. If an outsider who comes to visit us doesn't pay attention to our praying and what that means, then he'll miss the whole point."[26]

Next, we will pay attention to our praying.

CHAPTER THREE

PRAYERS

To pray is to open oneself to the possibility of sainthood, to the possibility of becoming set on fire by the Spirit.[1]

—KENNETH LEECH

Archaeologists have found some stones on a small mound, nestled at the end of a long valley shadowed by the hill country of Samaria, tantalizing remains of the first sanctuary ever built to the God of Israel. In the Bronze Age, pilgrims left the taxing labors of existence to pray and offer sacrifices to God in Shiloh. One woman prayed so persistently that she was brought to the attention of the priest, Eli. Misconstruing how utterly absorbed she was in her supplications, he upbraided her for showing up drunk. Hannah's reply was similar to Peter's on the day of Pentecost: "I have drunk neither wine nor strong drink, but I have been pouring out my soul before the Lord" (1 Sam. 1:15; see Acts 2:15).

I thought of this kind of intensive prayer several years ago when I visited a church named after Saint Augustine in Rome. The nave was dark, not ready for tourists. While my eyes struggled to adjust to the shadowy candlelight, I heard a plaintive, weeping voice, repeating over and over, "Mio bambino, mio bambino." A woman fervent in her prayer for her child was kneeling by the sarcophagus where the body of Saint Monica has rested for centuries. Monica was born in 331 and reared in a devout family. As wife and mother, she was resolute and unswerving in her faith. Her husband Patricius was unfaithful to her and exhibited a wicked temper. But her prayers and patience wrought a conversion in his soul, and he died a Christian.

Most of Monica's holy zeal was lavished on her son Augustine. Her dreams by night led her to believe he would be a great leader of the church. Wounded by day by her son's waywardness, she persisted in her dogged love for him and, above all, in her prayers for his soul and destiny. Seeing the passion of her supplications for him and somewhat vexed by her clinging and tears, the great bishop Ambrose told her, "Go away from me now. As you live, it is impossible that the son of such tears should perish."[2] For her this was an assurance from heaven. Augustine was converted and was baptized on Easter eve of 387. Indeed he did become a great saint and theologian, but Monica lived only a few weeks after his baptism, almost as if, having prayed her son to salvation, she could depart this earth in peace.

TERESA OF AVILA

Throughout history God has raised up a number of saints whose lives of prayer are exemplary for us—not so astonishing as to be unattainable but remarkably inviting and hopeful for us who forever are pleading, "Lord, teach us to pray." A Spanish girl named Teresa was born in Avila in March of 1515. Her father, Don Alonso Sánchez de Cepeda, was a nobleman of impeccable morals. So zealous was he that when he found pretty teenaged Teresa

Archivi Alinari-Firenze

The Ecstasy of St. Teresa by Bernini

engaging in some minor flirtation, he deposited her in a convent. She stuck with the cloistered life until her death in 1582—on October 4, the feast day of Saint Francis of Assisi. She had become a shrewd administrator and reformer within the Carmelite order in Spain, establishing fourteen houses of nuns.

A fragile young woman, Teresa often suffered life-threatening illnesses. In one stretch she lay virtually motionless for nearly three years. Either because of her wretched health or else in spite of it, she had frequent experiences when she heard voices and was elevated into a state of ecstasy, feeling herself ravished by the overwhelming presence of Christ. Her startling intimacy in prayer was forever captured in the Bernini sculpture in Rome, "The Ecstasy of St. Teresa." She saw angels and wrote with such depth and fervor that Pope Paul VI bestowed upon her the rare title, "Doctor of the Church," the only woman so honored. Legend suggests that she frequently had to cling to the altar rail during prayer to keep from floating upward.

Teresa's autobiography, *The Life of Teresa of Jesus*, is a religious classic and charts a memorable journey of progress in the life of prayer. A second classic, *The Interior*

Castle, is strange to modern eyes but probes the vastness of our unexplored selves. Her mapping of the steps to the life of prayer (self-knowledge, aiming at purity, renunciation, absorption into God, union, crucifixion of self, radiation of love, joy, and peace) is alluring and yet terribly elusive, at least for most of us.

For at one level, Teresa's religiosity seems alien. Surely only a few rare souls are gifted with such intensity in prayer. But at the heart of her relationship with God were two impulses without which we will never be close to God. The first is discipline, the regularity of reading, prayer, conversation and the sacraments. The second is an opening up of the emotional life to God. Desire is what must be captured if we are to be close to God. What we bring to God is not great holiness and wisdom but brokenness and profound need, a virtually desperate desire to be loved, held, and swept up into the very heart of God. Our weakness is not something to be corrected but becomes the crucible in which intimacy with God is established. When we expose our weakness, we understand what Teresa meant when she wrote, "God delivered me, in such a way that, even against my own will, He seems to have contrived that I should not be lost."[3] God is not somewhere far away, the object of some arduous quest or journey. Rather, God is very close, nearer to us than our next breath. This closeness is the theme of the life of another Teresa, three centuries later.

THÉRÈSE OF LISIEUX

In October of 1870, in the French village of Alençon, Zélie Martin buried her infant daughter, Thérèse, the fourth child she had lost in just three years. She and her husband Louis began to pray for another child, another "little

Thérèse," and on January 2, 1873, Zélie's prayers were answered. But she only enjoyed this child for four years. Despite having made a pilgrimage to the healing waters of Lourdes, Zélie died in 1877.

To her father's great credit, little Thérèse and her four older sisters enjoyed a loving, happy home that was open and passionate about the Christian life. When Thérèse was four, she loved to dress up as a nun and repeatedly said her greatest wish was to please Jesus. She was fascinated by saints, especially Joan of Arc, and always said she wished to be one. Having lost her mother, as well as four siblings, she had an eerie longing for heaven, where she might rejoin them. At fifteen she did join her living sisters in the Carmelite abbey in Lisieux as a happy participant in its daily rigor of six hours of prayer and five hours of manual labor.

Frail in health, Thérèse always sensed that her own death was never far away. This keen awareness of the fragility of life wrought in her a remarkable intimacy with God. When she was ten, she had a brief and beautiful vision of the virgin Mary. A year later, during a three-day retreat of prayer, she had an experience in which she was kissed by Jesus. In her autobiography, she described the moment:

> Ah, how sweet was that first kiss of Jesus! It was a kiss of love, I felt that I was loved, and I said: "I love you, and I give myself to you forever!" There were no requests, no struggles, no sacrifices; for a long time Jesus and poor little Thérèse looked at each other and understood each other. That day it was no longer simply a look, it was a fusion, there were no longer two, Thérèse had vanished like a drop of water lost in the depths of the ocean. Jesus alone remained. He was the Master, the King.[4]

Although Thérèse continued to endure painful losses in her life, she was no longer totally undone by them, so great was her sense of the love of Christ. Frequently and with no embarrassment, she kissed her crucifix right on the face. In words that are foreign to our ears, she grew more eager to die, for it was only in death that her consuming love for God could reach fruition. She prayed that God might take her without delay into the eternal embrace so that "I may be able to tell you of my love eternally face to face!"[5]

The language of Thérèse's journal reminds us that love for Christ can actually be much like the love in which we delight as people. Lovers ramble, saying foolish things. No renunciation is too great to achieve closeness with the beloved. Above the doorway to her room she carved, "Jesus is my only love." Love cannot be denied, even when it seemingly is not reciprocated. About times of pain and anguish she wrote, "My heaven is to smile at this God I adore when he is hiding and testing my love."[6]

The Little Way

Not surprisingly, poetry began to pour from Thérèse's heart:

> To die of love is what I hope for,
>   on fire with his love I want to be,
>   to see him, be one with him forever,
>   that is my heaven—that's my destiny:
>   by love to live.[7]

Thérèse exemplified to those around her the cruciality of seemingly trivial, small acts of love. She called it "the little way," partly indicating the simple deeds of love that are the life of holiness and also embodying the profound theological truth that God's power is revealed in our weakness. When no one would work with Sister Marie in the linen room, so fierce was her anger, Thérèse volunteered and loved her, just as Jesus must have loved all his disciples. So selfless was she that her sister Leonie once remarked that she had never seen Thérèse looking in a mirror.

She suffered mightily, a victim of tuberculosis. At the end of her life she claimed that she was falling into the arms of God. Moments before her death on September 30, she clutched her crucifix to her body and said, "Oh, I love you." She opened her eyes widely and looked straight up, making those near her believe it was her first clear glimpse into heaven. The year was 1897, the same year Dorothy Day (who would write a beautiful book about Thérèse) was born.

Interestingly, in the last weeks of her brief life, Thérèse sensed her work was not yet accomplished. She wished to remain active in heaven. "My mission is about to begin, my mission to make God loved as I love him, to give my little way to souls. If God grants my desires...I will spend my heaven doing good upon earth."[8] Indeed, within a decade her journal was translated into a dozen languages and soon sold over one million copies. Many readers were converted, and others were cured of diseases. In 1925, fewer than twenty-eight years after her death, Pope Pius XI canonized her as a saint. If we learn from her something about loving Jesus and "the little way," she indeed is still doing good upon the earth.

THE DEPTH OF WISDOM

We are blessed by many great pray-ers. In the fourteenth century a woman named Julian, a nun in Norwich, told of her mystical experiences of the cross of Christ in *Revelations of Divine Love* (a book also known as *Showings*). The fifteenth century produced the timeless devotional classic *The Imitation of Christ*, featuring those immortal words of Thomas à Kempis:

> Lord, in what can I trust in this life? And what is my greatest comfort on earth? Is it not Yourself, O Lord my God, whose mercy is limitless? Have I ever prospered without You? And did I ever suffer ill when You were at hand? I would rather be poor for Your sake than rich without You. I would choose to be a wanderer on the face of the earth with You, rather than to possess heaven without You. For where You are, there is Heaven; and where You are not, there is death and Hell. You are my sole desire; for You I sigh, pray, and cry....Unless You abide with me, all things that seem to bring peace and happiness are as nothing, for they cannot bestow true happiness. You alone are the End of all good things, the fullness of life, the depth of wisdom; and the greatest comfort of Your servants is to trust in You above all else. My God, Father of mercies, I look to You, I trust in You.[9]

In the sixteenth century, Ignatius Loyola, founder of the Jesuits, composed a workbook, a veritable exercise regimen for the soul, entitled the *Spiritual Exercises*, which many still use to envision scenes from the life of Christ and then deliberately try to embody them in real life. Thomas Cranmer taught generations of Anglicans to speak with God in flowering English through the pages of *The Book of Common Prayer*. In the seventeenth century Brother Lawrence worked in a kitchen in Paris, and he has taught us much about *The Practice of the Presence of God* (a book of his letters and thoughts). He urged us to look for God among the pots and pans, in every nook and cranny of our mundane lives. In every century witnesses have opened our eyes to the viability of the life of prayer. In *A Testament of Devotion*, Thomas

Kelly, a Quaker who died in 1941, told us about the sanctuary in our soul: "Eternity is at our hearts, pressing upon our time-torn lives, warming us with intimations of an astounding destiny, calling us home unto Itself."[10]

TWO MODERN GIANTS

At the end of our century, two giants of the spiritual life have towered above the rest: Thomas Merton and Henri Nouwen. Both were born in Europe, lived as Roman Catholics, were admired and loved by non-Catholics — and died prematurely. Merton was born in 1915 in France. His mother died when he was six, so he was reared by his father, a painter from New Zealand. They moved to Long Island, then back to France, before Thomas left to study literature in England. On December 10, 1941, he entered a Trappist monastery called Gethsemani in the hills of Kentucky, where he spent almost every day in work and contemplation until his death, twenty-six years later to the very day on a rare trip abroad in Bangkok.

Nouwen was deeply influenced by Merton, with whom he spoke only once, and briefly. Born in 1932 in the Netherlands, Nouwen became a priest at age twenty-five but thereafter studied psychology, first at Nijmegen and then at the Menninger Institute in Topeka, Kansas, blending theology with what science was learning about the inner life. After short teaching stints at Notre Dame and Utrecht, he was for a decade a professor at Yale and then spent two more years at Harvard — before a dramatic career shift, spending the last decade of his life working with severely handicapped adults. Tragically and in an eerie way like Merton, Nouwen died on an overseas trip on September 21, 1996, in Amsterdam.

THOMAS MERTON

In a sense, Merton and Nouwen devised no clever strategies, no nine easy-to-follow steps, no recipe for success in the life of prayer. Instead, both of them bared their own souls in a way that unveiled to us how the presence of God is not a small compartment of our lives but actually pervades all of life. Merton's best-known book is *The Seven Storey Mountain*, an autobiographical narrative (covering Merton's life through 1948) that is totally candid without being self-indulgent, in some ways akin to the *Confessions* of Saint Augustine. With humility Merton holds up his own struggles and uses them the way we use curtains — something to be grasped, then drawn back, so we may look out into the light.

He spoke amusingly of how his soul was tortured in early youth by a pretty girl — and how his passion for academics cloaked his deep insecurity. As he watched his father's body being ravaged by cancer, he poignantly wrote,

> Souls are like athletes, that need opponents worthy of them, if they are to be tried and extended and pushed to the full use of their powers, and rewarded according to their capacity. And my father was in a fight with this tumor, and none of us understood the battle. We thought he was done for, but it was making him great. And I think God was already weighing out to him the weight of reality that was to be his reward.[11]

When his brother, John Paul, was killed over the North Sea in 1943, Merton wrote an emotional poem that included the line, "For in the wreckage of your April Christ lies slain, / And Christ weeps in the ruins of my spring."[12] He also heard the weeping of Christ and dared to name it during the civil rights movement and in the midst of protests against the war in Vietnam.

Merton's interest in the Far East extended beyond the war. Surprisingly to many Catholics, he listened to and developed a profound appreciation for the religions of the Orient, especially Zen Buddhism. While never thinking for a moment, as so many do today, that all religions are the same, he did discern how the methodology of Zen, especially the emptying of the self, can open Christian eyes to "all forms of delusion arising out of spiritual ambition and self-complacency which aim to establish the ego in spiritual glory."[13]

Playing the Prodigal

Reading Merton can be like undergoing radical surgery to the soul. For he was a great diagnostician of the human condition—which is interesting, given the restricted inter-action he actually had with people beyond his monastery walls. Yet Merton illustrates that the monk, whose life is built around solitude, has not withdrawn from the world so much as he has stepped back from the world to see it more clearly and to lift it up into the care of God.

If we pay attention, those of us who are not monks dis-cover that the routines and noises and busy schedules of our everyday life distract us from prayer and actually sup-port our waywardness, much as a spouse can cloak her beloved's alcoholism. As Merton said, we can play the prodigal son very well without ever running away from home. Watching television, for instance, becomes a dan-gerous inversion of the life of contemplation, substituting passivity, inertia, and uncritical absorption for the kind of active, probing, obedient reflection that is prayer.

Our sense of freedom in daily life is mere delusion. The sad, ironic truth is that we get trapped in the regimen dic-tated to us by an ungodly world. Over time and tragically, we settle into a dismal satisfaction with our busy-ness as our passion for higher things is dulled or forgotten. God then is rightly perceived as a threat to the security into which we have been lulled. "Much of our coldness and dry-ness in prayer may well be a kind of unconscious defense against grace."[14]

Spirituality begins in letting those defenses down in the brutal truth of self-discovery. For, inside the self-seeking soul there is, quite literally, nothing.

> I use up my life in the desire for pleasures and the thirst of experiences, for power, honor, knowledge and love, to clothe this false self and construct its nothingness into something objectively real. And I wind experiences around myself and cover myself with pleasures and glory like bandages in order to make myself perceptible to myself and to the world, as if I were an invisible body that could only become visible when something visible covered its surface.
>
> But there is no substance under the things with which I am clothed. I am hollow....And when they are gone there will be nothing left of me but my own naked-ness and emptiness and hollowness, to tell me that I am my own mistake.[15]

Merton's devotional classic *New Seeds of Contemplation* explores this theme of how we pretend to be what we are not. A bogus self usurps our lives and strangles our desire, so that we no longer desire God at all, or only dimly so.

Beginners All Our Life

Prayer is about recovering our true identity. Being a saint is simply being yourself. A relationship with God is pure gift, all from God's side. But we must avail ourselves of this gift. Merton's daily routine in the cloister underlined his sense of the importance of discipline, of worship, of the sacraments. These are crucial, for in the usual routine of life, we get virtually desensitized to the things of God, tasting of the goods the world has to offer, and, over time, lowering our sights. By the practice of prayer, we prepare for the coming of God. As a gift, it is something for which we can only wait. But there is a decision to be made, requiring not only discipline but also love.

> The fact remains that contemplation will not be given to those who wilfully remain at a distance from God, who confine their interior life to a few routine exercises of piety and a few external acts of worship and service performed as a matter of duty. Such people are careful to avoid sin. They respect God as a Master. But their heart does not belong to Him. They are not really interested in Him, except in order to insure themselves against losing heaven and going to hell. In actual practice, their minds and hearts are taken up with their own ambitions and troubles and comforts and pleasures and all their worldly interests and anxieties and fears. God is only invited to enter this charmed circle to smooth out difficulties and to dispense rewards.[16]

Being oneself, rediscovering one's deepest identity, requires intense effort—and help. If we are at all serious about drawing closer to God, we need someone who can ruthlessly pull up the rugs and look behind things to reveal accumulated dust and grime in our souls. Guilt is not merely a neurotic form of anxiety. It is all too real. We truly have defected from God and leaped across a chasm into the darkness of estrangement. A whole lifetime will never be enough to remove all the obstacles between our hearts and God—so we must be patient, expecting that "we will never be anything else but beginners, all our life!"[17] But that life as a beginner, while a valiant struggle, is a great joy, somehow being in sync with the genuine person we were made to be.

Evil does not vanish from our lives. And yet, evil is not to be dwelled upon. A clever chapter in *New Seeds of Contemplation* is entitled "The Moral Theology of the Devil." Merton wryly suggests that the devil has a very persuasive kind of theology: that the world is evil, that we are evil, that life is about obedience to laws, that the threat of punishment looms to motivate us to do good, that we must watch out at every moment for the devil and his deeds. And for all who have known Christians who seem to know and talk quite a bit about the devil, Merton concludes,

> Finally, as might be expected, the moral theology of the devil grants an altogether unusual amount of importance to…the devil. Indeed one soon comes to find out that he is the very center of the whole system. That he is behind everything. That he is moving everybody in the world except ourselves. That he is out to get even with us. And that there is every chance of his doing so because, it now appears, his power is equal to that of God.[18]

A sign of growth in holiness is that we think less and less about what is evil. Merton wrote that "the saint is never offended by anything and judges no man's sin because he does not know sin. He knows the mercy of God. He knows that his own mission on earth is to bring that mercy to all."[19]

HENRI NOUWEN

As Merton fulfilled that mission, so did a somewhat younger man, another European Catholic who lived much of his life in America. As a child Henri Nouwen loved to dress up and pretend to be a priest; he never wanted to be anything else. From 1969 until 1996 he was a priest to untold thousands of readers, giving us more than three dozen books, each one remarkable for its simplicity and beauty.

Nouwen wrote about the life of prayer and about the ministry, about aging and about families, about growing up and about dying. For me his prayers, those printed in books like *Cry for Mercy* and *Heart Speaks to Heart*, are the prayers I have wanted and needed to pray, not always having been able to find the words. Nouwen went places I wished to go, thought thoughts I would need more time to have thought, explored regions of the soul I have been afraid to explore.

Basically he wrote about his life, but not in any self-indulgent way. He assumed his thoughts and desires were normal. As he contemplated his life in the light of God's love and call, he helped us to understand our own lives as belonging to God. He wrote about a sabbatical he took in Rome and about a journey to Latin America. He wrote about his mother's death and about a brush he had with death. He told about special people he knew and let us peek over his shoulder as he went about talking with God.

Open Hands

Hands figure prominently in Nouwen's writing. He begins *With Open Hands*, a great little invitation to the spiritual life, by reminding us that "the resistance to praying is like the resistance of tightly clenched fists." Near the end of *Here and Now: Living in the Spirit* he uses the image of hands to characterize the possibilities in a marriage, how instead of gripping each other tensely, hands (and therefore people) may gently touch, as if in prayer, leaving space for God and for others. And perhaps his wisest and most moving book is an extended meditation on Rembrandt's painting *The Return of the Prodigal Son*, in which the father's strong and gentle hands embrace a worn-out young man longing for home.

When we dig into Nouwen's legacy, asking of him,

"Teach us to pray," it is striking that he never talks about prayer as a mechanism he deployed, successfully or unsuccessfully, to get God to do this or that. Prayer for him was a pouring out of his heart with blatant honesty to God, and at the same time a listening to God, stretching out to hear God's whisperings of love, bracing to hear God's call. In the middle of his whirlwind life of travel, speaking, and writing, Nouwen always took time for solitude and prayer. In the second half of 1974 he took a sabbatical from Yale at a Trappist monastery, the Abbey of the Genesee in Piffard, New York. Immersed in totally silent solitude and physically removed from the busy routines of life in the world, Nouwen learned (and shared with us in *The Genesee Diary*) how we truly are alone; how we need, yet fear, silence; how God is present in surprising ways, not just when we are in retreat from the world but in the midst of the busy-ness of life as we know it.

Road to Daybreak

Nouwen's diary of his year in Trosly at the l'Arche community was published as *The Road to Daybreak*. Nouwen, seemingly on top of the world, tenured and famous at Harvard, at age fifty-three was restless, dissatisfied. Something he could not even define was missing. The fact that a spiritual giant like Nouwen could admit to being in such a fix offers hope to the rest of us. More remarkably, he did something about it, something pretty unusual—and while that may be threatening to us, it is surely even more hopeful.

✳ Seven years earlier a woman named Jan Risse had ✳ showed up one day and brought him greetings from Jean Vanier. Nouwen was struck by this seemingly unimportant message and was unsure why. Years later Vanier met Nouwen in Chicago for a time of silent prayer, then invited

Nouwen to visit him in France. Intrigued, Nouwen realized "that Jan Risse's visit had been the first of a series of events in which Jesus was responding to my prayer to follow him more fully."[20] At the l'Arche community for mentally handicapped adults in Trosly, Nouwen said,

> I experienced a sense of homeness I had not experienced at Yale, in Latin America, or at Harvard. The noncompetitive life with mentally handicapped people, their gifts of welcoming me regardless of name or prestige, and the persistent invitation to "waste some time" with them opened in me a place that until then had remained unavailable to me, a place where I could hear the gentle invitation of Jesus to dwell with him.[21]

To the amazement and even disappointment of the world, Nouwen resigned from Harvard. After a year in France, he moved on to become pastor of the Daybreak community outside Toronto, where he spent the balance of his life in ministry with six handicapped men. This shift is stunning in many ways. Nouwen proved that God's call is not along some upwardly mobile track as measured by the world. God wanted Nouwen, not at Harvard but by the bedside of Adam, a single, severely disabled man.

> My decision to leave Harvard was a difficult one. For many months I was not sure if I would be following or betraying my vocation by leaving. The outer voices kept saying, 'You can do so much good here. People need you!' The inner voices kept saying, 'What good is it to preach the Gospel to others while losing your own soul?' Finally, I realized that my increasing inner darkness, my feelings of being rejected by some of my students, colleagues, friends, and even God, my inordinate need for affirmation and affection, and my deep sense of not belonging were clear signs that I was not following the way of God's spirit. The fruits

of the spirit are not sadness, loneliness, and separation, but joy, solitude, and community. After I decided to leave Harvard, I was surprised that it had taken me so long to come to that decision. As soon as I left, I felt so much inner freedom, so much joy and new energy, that I could look back on my former life as a prison in which I had locked myself. [22]

Nouwen espoused no heroic view of his move. We might apply the "saint" category to him for this kind of selfless devotion, but he claimed he was doing it for himself. Perhaps being a saint is like that: The best thing we can do for ourselves is what God calls us to do, no matter what anyone else might think. The spiritual life is, above all, about calling. And the call can be to the most surprising places, where we most surely see God, as in the "gift of the handicapped": "They see through a façade of smiles and friendly words and sense the resentful heart before we ourselves notice it. Often they are capable of unmasking our impatience, irritation, jealousy, and lack of interest and making us honest with ourselves. For them, what really counts is a true relationship, a real friendship, a faithful presence." [23]

LESSONS OF PRAYER

If we would pray with Hannah and Nouwen, with Teresa and Merton, we need to relearn from them what prayer is—and isn't. Prayer isn't something pasted onto an otherwise irreligious day, but it permeates everything we do. Prayer is not something we do because it "works." Whether it works or not is utterly unimportant to the saints. For them prayer is all about love, the creation of communion with the God from whom the soul cannot bear to be apart.

Proper technique is not prayer. As Thérèse of Lisieux wrote about her praying: "I say nothing to him, I love him."[24]

Even when we pray for others, it is all about love, togetherness. When Monica died, Augustine touchingly wrote, "I closed her eyes, and a mighty sorrow welled up from the depths of my heart....my heart was wounded through and my life as if ripped asunder. For out of her life and mine one life had been made."[25] Prayer joins my life to the life of God, and it joins my life to others, all of it really just one life. Brother Roger, founder of Taizè, whose worship and music have transformed churches and countless lives and who is regarded as a saint by many, was quoted in *Time* as saying, "We should not pray for any useful end, but in order to create a community of free men with Christ." Prayer has its effects — precisely because in some mysterious way our lives become one.

THE ONLY WAY TO PRAY

Prayer doesn't just happen. It is a matter of discipline. All the saints pray, regularly and deliberately, building prayer squarely and irrevocably into their daily schedules. Nouwen loved to quote Dom John Chapman, who said, "The only way to pray is to pray; and the way to pray well is to pray much."[26] No single regimen, no particular gimmick, can claim to be "the" way to God. Different disciplines work for different people, and what works at one stage of life may need to be discarded for another way at a later stage. But for all the saints, prayer is the most important part of any day. Prayer cannot be crowded out. It is the "one thing needful" (Luke 10:38-42, AP).

Prayer is never easy, and in this life we never achieve a perfect communion with God. Even Thérèse of Lisieux had great bouts of spiritual hollowness, times when she doubted God, as if she were thrashing up against a wall. Yet the fact that we are still in a flawed world where unalloyed union with God is impossible reminds us that prayer does not remove us from reality but immerses us in it, calling us into service, toward tangible expressions of our love for God. Karl Barth reminded us that prayer is the beginning of an uprising against the disorder of the world. Prayer is about hearing our calling, a calling into the fray, taking God's side in a high-stakes battle.

Consider how many of the saints we have studied were frail of body, suffering ill health, hovering near death. Their lesson to us is that when it comes down to life and death, when we take stock of what really matters, our relationship with God pushes its way to the forefront. We may heed the advice of Joseph Cardinal Bernardin, who advised us (during his bout with cancer): "Pray while you're well, because if you wait until you're sick you might not be able to do it."[27]

Whether we are in good health or in mortal fragility, prayer is the beginning and anticipation of a lasting relationship with God. There is a story about Thomas Aquinas, one of the greatest theologians in the history of the church. Born in 1225 to a noble Lombard family, he preferred to listen rather than to talk; being rather on the obese side, he was nicknamed "the dumb ox." But on his deathbed he displayed true wisdom. Friends hovering nearby heard a voice from above: "You have spoken well of me; what reward would you like?" And this author of dozens of magisterial volumes of dogma replied, "Nothing but Yourself, Lord."[28] It is to teachers much like Thomas Aquinas we now turn.

CHAPTER FOUR

TEACHERS

Tradition is democracy extended through time. Tradition means giving the vote to the most obscure of all classes, our ancestors. Tradition is the democracy of the dead. Tradition refuses to submit to the small and arrogant oligarchy of those who are walking about.[1]

—G. K. CHESTERTON

Great Christian teachers like Thomas Aquinas have seen themselves not so much as innovators, thinkers of previously unconceived thoughts, but as interpreters, those who have clutched an ancient and precious treasure to their hearts and have dared to say something about it, humbly to question it, and openly to be questioned by it. Hebrews 11 rehearses in grand fashion virtually the table of contents of that treasure, the stories of the life of God and God's people in ancient Israel. The Gospels are the reply to the child's request, "Tell me the stories of Jesus." Paul was the forefather and the greatest of all the teachers who plumbed the depths of those stories and who were bold enough to say, "Today, now, for you and me, God is like this; God is saying this; God is doing this." Gregory Thaumaturgus set the standard when he described his teacher, Origen: "This man has received from God the greatest gift and from heaven the better part; he is the interpreter of the words of God...he understands the things of God as if God were speaking to him and he explains them...that [all] may understand them.[2]

KARL BARTH

At the seemingly impossible reach of nineteen hundred years from the founding of the church, a wise teacher of theology clarified what is at stake for the Christian teacher. "We ought to speak of God. We are human, however, and so cannot speak of God. We ought therefore to recognize both our obligation and our inability

Archive Photos

and by that very recognition give God the glory. This is our perplexity."[3] Karl Barth, probably the greatest theological teacher of the twentieth century, for all his genius, knew that knowledge consisted in knowing that God far exceeds all that we can think about the divine.

Barth was born in Basel, May 10, 1886. His father Fritz and his grandfather were theologians, his mother Anna the daughter of a pastor. After studies in Berlin, Tübingen, and Marburg, he became an assistant pastor in Geneva and married Nelly Hoffman, a member of his first confirmation class. In 1911 he became a pastor in Safenwil. He was dumbfounded by the misery of workers in the region and focused heavily on social issues. But the horrors of World War I drove him back to the Bible. In part his dramatic shift came in August 1914 when German theologians, including some of his own teachers, issued statements supporting the aggressive war policy of Wilhelm II.

In 1916 Barth embarked on an intensive study of Romans, setting out to read it as if he had never heard it before and as if no scholarship dissecting it existed. His reading and reflections issued in notebook after notebook, handwritten, a paraphrase of Romans, which appeared in book form in 1919. In this commentary on the Epistle to the Romans, Barth spoke of how, as we rethink and wrestle with Paul's words, the walls that separate us from the first century become transparent.

The Massive Bell Ringing

So provocative was his reading of Paul that the theological world was shaken; more surprising is that churches and believers around the world also felt the impact of his thought. Barth was so surprised that he said it was as if he had felt his way up the stairs of a dark church tower and, trying to steady himself, unexpectedly caught hold of a bell-rope instead of the handrail and was shocked to hear the massive bell ringing above his head.

The bell he rang was this: He reminded us that theology, that Christianity itself, is about God. Too often we nestle into a brand of Christianity that zeroes in on "me as a Christian," "my beliefs," "how I feel," "how I am saved," "my walk with God." Fascinating as our lives and feelings may be, God is infinitely more interesting, and we are made by God to think about God, for God is God. There is a God, and "one can *not* speak of God simply by speaking of man in a loud voice."[4]

The basis of our faith is not a feeling but a fact, something that happened, a definitive revelation of God in time. Shortly before he died in December 1968 (on the very day that Thomas Merton died!), Barth said, "The last word which I have to say as a theologian and also as a politician is not a term like 'grace,' but a name, 'Jesus Christ.' He is grace, and he is the last, beyond the world and the church and even theology.... What I have been concerned to do in my long life has been increasingly to emphasize this name."[5]

For Barth what God revealed to us through Jesus Christ is everything. Nothing within prepares us to know God; on our own we may think clever thoughts, but we only know God because God in an unexpected flash of mercy is revealed through the pages of scripture. The Bible is not God. We do not worship the Bible but the one to whom the Bible bears witness.

Barth's passion was not primarily scholarship, criticism, or learning but love for the Lord Jesus. Hanging over his desk for over sixty years was a copy of Matthias Grünewald's painting of the crucifixion from the Isenheim Altarpiece, gruesome yet inviting, arresting yet hopeful, in which the long finger of John the Baptist points to the Crucified. Barth wanted to be that finger.

This desire profoundly influenced the way Barth lived. His refusal to take an oath of allegiance to Adolf Hitler in 1934, was not a political statement but a theological declaration that there is one God only. He was dismissed from his teaching position and exiled from Germany because of that refusal. During his years of teaching in Basel, few knew that each year on Christmas Day, he left his family and went to the local prison to preach sermons that reveal his astonishing belief in the power of God's word, his hope for all people, his commitment to Christ's great commission.

There is a humility about Barth, who recognized that every human doctrine about God, every attempted formulation, is flawed and correctable. He gave glory to God through his *Church Dogmatics*, which stretched into a dozen massive volumes, each brilliant and eloquent. As great as this achievement was and continues to be, he wisely remarked that "in heaven we shall know all that is necessary, and we shall not have to write on paper or read any more. Indeed, I shall be able to dump even the *Church Dogmatics*, over the growth of which the angels have long been amazed, on some heavenly floor as a pile of waste paper."[6] His eleven honorary doctorates, in the same way, would have to be handed in at the cloakroom.

For every Barth, the kind of teacher who can produce massive tomes of truth in its wondrous complexity, there needs to be a C. S. Lewis, the sort of teacher who can communicate in a compelling way with the masses, reaching not just grownups but also children through spellbinding books, witty lectures, and even the media.

CLIVE STAPLES LEWIS

Born in Belfast on November 29, 1898,[7] Lewis lost his mother, Flora, to cancer just before his tenth birthday. As a teenager he went off to school at Oxford, was injured in France in World War I—and lost his faith. In 1929 his father Albert also died of cancer. A few weeks later Lewis was converted, and no one was more surprised than Lewis himself. "I gave in, admitted that God was God, and knelt and prayed; perhaps, that night, the most dejected and reluctant convert in all England."[8]

While a professor of literature at Oxford, he founded the Inklings, a tightly knit group of thinkers and writers including J. R. R. Tolkien, Charles Williams, and Owen Barfield. Truth was their passion, writing their vehicle. For three decades they met regularly for discussion and to read books they were working on out loud to one another. Just imagine: on Tuesday mornings during 1937, these friends listened to Tolkien's rough draft, section by section, of *The Lord of the Rings*. Charles Williams read his *All Hallows' Eve*. Before *The Screwtape Letters* appeared in serial form in *The Guardian*, Lewis read each section aloud to his friends. They must have been awed.

The year was 1940. Lewis's brother, "Warnie," had been evacuated from Dunkirk. The Nazi blitzkrieg threatened civilization; Lewis heard a Hitler harangue on the radio and had no doubt that evil was a reality. With charming levity mingled with deadly seriousness, Lewis artfully penned these letters, purportedly the correspondence among the demons: "There are two equal and opposite errors into which our race can fall about the devils. One is to disbelieve in their existence. The other is to believe, and to feel an excessive and unhealthy interest in them. They themselves are equally pleased by both errors, and hail a materialist or a magician with the same delight."[9]

The Screwtape Letters has for more than a half century been a bestseller and one that has genuinely done many people a lot of good, helping them to understand their inner life, how they slide unawares into the grasp of banality, how temptation wages its sneaky and alluring battle for the soul.

As Lewis's renown grew, so did the demand for his words. In 1941, he gave a series of talks on the BBC, something of a basic apology for and explanation of Christianity that we know as the book *Mere Christianity*. As a college student I read *Mere Christianity*, and it had a powerful impact on me, igniting my curiosity to think about my own faith far more thoroughly. Instead of sitting in an ivory tower weighing the academic quandaries of the day, Lewis tried to answer the real questions real people had about the faith. *The Problem of Pain* tried to tackle why a good God permits suffering. *Miracles* strove to answer skeptics who sprawled over the stumbling block of the miraculous in the Bible. Another serial in *The Guardian* (published later as *The Great Divorce*) took an imaginative view of the existence of hell. And Lewis narrated his own hell in *A Grief Observed*, a poignant gathering of his thoughts after the death of Joy Davidman Gresham, his wife for just four years, lost (like his mother) to cancer in 1960.

Lewis breathed his life into another medium, the novel. His trilogy, *Out of the Silent Planet*, *Perelandra*, and *That Hideous Strength*, published between 1938 and 1945, proved to be not just terrific science fiction but also narratives of the triumph of good over evil. Many people regard The Chronicles of Narnia as the finest children's books ever written. Aslan, the magnificent creature in *The Lion, the Witch, and the Wardrobe*, transparently plays the part of Christ, awakening in children's minds the drama of the life, death, and resurrection of our Lord. To critics who poked fun at him for writing in this genre, he replied, "Critics who treat *adult* as a term of approval...cannot be adult themselves. To be concerned about being grown up..., to blush at the suspicion of being childish; these things are the marks of childhood and adolescence."[10] Lewis retained a childlike innocence and playfulness throughout his life and work. He died a true saint of our century on the same day as John F. Kennedy, November 22, 1963, but lives on in his immensely popular books.

AUGUSTINE OF HIPPO

To many, the greatest teacher of any century was Saint Augustine.[11] He was born in 354 in the town of Thagaste, in what today is Algeria. His father, Patricius, was a hard man with a hot temper. His mother, Monica, has become the patron saint of lost, wayward children. As brilliant a mental prodigy as her son became, his sampling from the smorgasbord of Mediterranean intellectual life led him erratically in every conceivable direction, and not just intellectually. At seventeen, just after his father's death, he took a concubine and never disclosed her name in writing. They had a son, Adeodatus. Augustine broke his mother's heart, most of all because of his beliefs, as he drifted among flavors of philosophical speculation in Carthage, Rome, and then Milan.

Fortunately, in Milan his fertile thirty-year-old mind encountered the great bishop, Ambrose, who set Augustine on a quest that culminated in the summer of 386. For years Augustine had prayed to God, "Give me chastity, but not yet." His wait ended abruptly in the garden of Alypius when his anxiety-riddled soul heard a voice, saying "Take up and read." He picked up a Bible and read, "Not in revelling and drunkenness, not in lust or wantonness, but arm yourself in the Lord Jesus, and spend no more thought on nature's appetites." The rest is history. He was baptized, ordained shortly thereafter, and was not long in becoming bishop of Hippo in Northern Africa, where he served thirty-five years until his death in 430. As he breathed his last, delving one last time into his book of Psalms, the Vandals were overrunning the Roman empire, banging at the gates of his own city of Hippo.

Through his preaching, and mostly for us through his

writing, Augustine clarified once and for all how we think about several crucial issues, each of which still has a tremendous bearing on how we function as Christians today. He tackled the mystery of the Trinity, predestination, and the thorniest passages of the Bible. He debated some of the great thinkers of his day and did so in front of great crowds, even in the public baths. For the moment, we want to look at what he taught us about sin and salvation, about love for God, and also about the church.

The Battle for Human Nature

Augustine taught us, better than anyone in history, about who we are way down deep as we grope about after God. And he spoke not just abstractly about people in general. He told us the intimate struggles of his own life in the great spiritual classic the *Confessions*, a book that can serve as a mirror that enables us to look with astonishing clarity into our own souls. He wrote it around 397, just as he was battling what we call "middle age."

At the core of our being, we are lovers. The problem is that our love gets misdirected; it lunges out after unworthy objects of affection. Our predicament as people is that we are, spiritually speaking, incompetent, beleaguered by contradictions. As Charles Williams restated Augustine's thought, we are not so much "in" a situation as we "are" a situation. Try as we might, we are never able to conquer those untamed cravings and unholy yearnings. We remain "prone to wander." A single sin is repeated, which becomes a habit; and we are utterly unable to "just say no." Even the good that we do, on close inspection, is polluted with selfish motives.

Just as Augustine was realizing the scope of our entanglement in sin, another brilliant teacher, Pelagius, a transplant from Britain, was enthralling crowds in Rome—but with a variant theology that would strike most modern people as somehow correct, were it not for Augustine himself. To Pelagius, we are able to do good, to choose what is right. Perfection is possible, and therefore obligatory. Pelagius did not forget the grace of God; but to him grace is precisely the gift of being able to do what God has commanded. He scoffed at the very idea of "original sin." We sin, indeed, but we can do better. Pelagius read the *Confessions*—and was profoundly disturbed.

Some have suggested that Pelagius misconstrued the human predicament in part because he had no children! Augustine grasped the perversity of our nature, perhaps from watching little Adeodatus, but primarily from his own memories of childhood: little thieveries, gross and total selfishness. He also knew from cradling Adeodatus, the humbling yet beautiful dependence of babies on their parents; such is our life in the hands of God.

Pelagius also failed to grasp the pressures, the systemic environment that hopelessly compromises all of us. If I decide today, "I am not going to be materialistic any longer," this resolve will last as long as I live in the United States for no more than a couple of waking hours. We are just so enmeshed in the culture. To Pelagius evil is a tough but beatable foe. But surely Augustine was a more subtle thinker, a more realistic perceiver. He knew that the dark specter of evil is not to be trifled with, that there are forces on the loose that can seize individuals and even whole cultures by the throat and squeeze the very life out of them.

Worst of all, Pelagius minimized the cruciality of Christ. Pelagius seemed to lay the burden of salvation squarely upon the individual. And nothing is sadder and more hopeless than being required to shoulder the responsibility for salvation when you look in the mirror and see someone with what T. S. Eliot called "shabby equipment always deteriorating." For Augustine, Christ existed not so much as an example to us (although no higher or better example could ever exist) but primarily to save us precisely when we fail to follow that perfect example. And that "when" was years ago; it was just a few minutes ago; it is now; it will be tomorrow morning as well. In one sense there is no "cure" for sin, yet there is a remedy that does not rest in my determination but is mingled in the blood flowing from the wounds of Jesus on the cross.

The Nature of God's Love

The dispute between these two giants, who never met face to face, was hotly contested and observed with great interest by Christians around the Mediterranean; riots broke out in the streets! Augustine won the day, not so much because of his great rhetorical skills or cleverness in argument, but rather because he spoke the truth, a truth not immediately evident, a truth that is still hard to hear, being so humbling and downright embarrassing, and yet for precisely that reason so honest and liberating and hopeful.

For the banner that flies over all of Christendom is the grace of God, the free gift of hope, the unmerited love that God eagerly showers on us that strikes us as so marvelous precisely because of the shabbiness of our condition. Love that is earned is not love. And the unmerited love of God provokes love in return. Love for God is not some duty but the reflex of the heart that knows it is unconditionally surrounded by mercy. Grace is the gift of freedom, of inner transformation.

Augustine taught us a crucial distinction that can and must refine and reshape what we mean when we say we "love" God. In the Latin culture of the fourth century, there were two kinds of love, *uti* and *frui*. *Uti* is the love of use. I love money, not in and of itself, not because I want to fondle it in my hands, but because I can use it for something else I really want. *Frui* is the love of enjoyment. I love chocolate, not because I use it for something else; actually, what I "use" it for (raising my cholesterol, fattening my belly) isn't so good — but I still love chocolate and will do anything to get it, to savor it. This distinction applies to people: We don't want to be used by someone. We want to be loved, just for who we are, quite apart from what we may or may not have done lately. In the same way, God does not exist to be used by us, although we certainly go at God with this motive all the time, hoping to co-opt God to help us get something we really want. God wants to be loved, to be enjoyed, no matter the cost.

The Nature of the Church

Christians in Augustine's day knew this cost. In Northern Africa the Donatist churches, with their insightful interpreter of the Bible, Tyconius, were zealous for the truth and energetic in doing good. Their grave concern was with Christians who had "lapsed" during times of persecution. Many church leaders had even collaborated with Diocletian's persecutors just a few decades earlier; others had renounced their faith under pressure. To the Donatists those priests were forever tainted. And therefore, their work was invalid. That meant that those they baptized or ordained and the churches they established were also invalidated.

The Donatists underlined boldly the need for the church to be holy, to practice what it preaches. Rightly they clung to a vision of commitment to goodness, fearing that if sin were lightly forgiven and accepted, the church would be imperiled. But Augustine struggled toward a different kind of church, one that could strive for holiness while recognizing the inevitable presence of sin, a holiness that need not separate from the world but remain fully immersed in the real life of the world. Basically he argued that the great rites of the church (baptism, the Lord's Supper) did not depend on the holiness of the minister who performed those rites but rather depended wholly upon God. There is no "pure" church; no band of Christians ever qualify as some kind of spiritual elite. We are, as Karl Barth said, always "amateurs," always sinners in need of grace.

A Lighted Match

Centuries passed. Augustine was hailed as the greatest "doctor," the church's wisest teacher, read and interpreted and translated and updated throughout Christendom. The only thing that matched the beauty of his comprehension of the grace of God was the ongoing proof that he was right about the resiliency of sin, even in the church. By the sixteenth century, much of what went on in the church had become a travesty, a comic perversion of its true self. Bishops, cardinals, and popes purchased their positions. Celibacy was mere pretense.

Squandering all the church money on sumptuous living, Pope Leo X was virtually broke by 1517. Cleverly he announced a special sale, a "jubilee" of indulgences. Christians were granted the opportunity to pay money to reduce the penalties for sin on behalf of the dead, and even of those still alive, all to rebuild Saint Peter's in Rome. Leo had a cathedral to rebuild, and there were geniuses (Michelangelo, Titian, and Raphael) to be pampered. Church bureaucrats like Johann Tetzel used music and jugglers and bogus relics of saints in something of a traveling circus to raise cash. Charles Williams was right about this bizarre idea for fundraising: "Unfortunately whoever thought of it dropped a lighted match into that unknown cellar of man's mind which contains the heavily dynamic emotions known as 'faith' and 'works.'"[12]

MARTIN LUTHER

The particular mind that ignited the Reformation belonged to Martin Luther.[13] At high noon on October 31, 1517, this then unheard-of professor of Old Testament in Wittenburg nailed ninety-five theses to the door of the parish church. The firestorm that ensued provoked Pope Leo to observe all too truly, a bull that included this prayer: "Arise, O Lord, and judge thy cause. A wild boar has invaded thy vineyard."[14]

This boar was born on November 10, 1483. Luther's parents, Hans and Margaret, lived quiet lives in Eisleben. His plans to become a lawyer were struck to the ground along with his person in a thunderstorm one summer day in 1505; he was twenty-one. Fearing for his life, he cried out, "St. Anne help me! I will become a monk."[15]

And a monk above all other monks Luther became, so zealous was his dogged pursuit of holiness. Regimented prayers, frequent fasting, coarse clothing, and mortification of the body were more than just his daily routine; they were attempts to reach upward toward God out of sinful human misery, desperate lunges to make up for offenses against a wrathful God who tolerates no sin. No monk surpassed Luther in zeal for righteousness; as he wrote later, "If ever a monk got to heaven by his monkery it was I."[16]

Yet that zeal was Luther's undoing; the unreachability

of a life wholly and purely devoted to God left him exasperated. Fortunately he had a wise pastor, one John Staupitz, who sensed Luther's distress. "Look here, if you expect Christ to forgive you, come in with something to forgive—parricide, blasphemy, adultery—instead of all these peccadilloes!"[17] said Staupitz, who comforted and encouraged the overly scrupulous Luther, pointing him to the wounds of Christ as proofs of God's love and compassion. Since Luther's job was the teaching of Bible, he kept reading and thinking and reading more in that Bible. In 1513 he lectured on Psalms, then in 1516 on Galatians.

Often throughout history, reading the Bible has proved to be dangerous, a grave threat to the status quo, no more so than with this sensitive professor of Old Testament. What he heard from that Bible and the way it clashed with current church practice, drove him to nail those theses on the Wittenburg door and to dare to offend the emperor. "We should rear living temples, ...and last of all St. Peter's." "[The pope] would do better to sell Saint Peter's and give the money to the poor folk who are being fleeced by the hawkers of indulgences."[18]

Here I Stand

Little wonder the powers that be panicked. Luther's books were banned and burned—and therefore read all the more eagerly by Christians hungry for change. Summoned to stand trial before the Diet of Worms, Luther was shown a pile of his books: "Are these yours?" "The books are all mine," he proudly claimed and then characteristically added, "and I have written more."[19] To the demand that he repudiate his books and all he was preaching and teaching, Luther boldly stood up to the arrayed might of the Holy Roman Empire and the pope's legates: "My conscience is captive to the Word of God. I cannot and I will not recant anything, for to go against conscience is neither right nor safe. Here I stand, I cannot do otherwise. God help me."[20]

Banished by the church, Luther hid for a time in the Wartburg castle; having grown a beard, he pretended to be a knight. While in hiding he translated the whole New Testament into German. Luther's teaching was not just for scholars and not just for the political fray. He wanted to put the word of God into the hands of every person—and did so. Fortunately and providentially, Luther's translating came at that turning point in history marked by the advent of the printing press—and thousands of Bibles with wood-cut illustrations became available, altering forever the entire mental approach people brought to their faith.

Immediately the worship services in Germany were transformed. On Christmas Eve of 1521, with Andreas Carlstadt filling in at the Castle Church for Luther, worshipers heard for the first time in their lives the words "the body and blood of Christ" in their native tongue. Luther produced catechisms, focusing on the Apostles' Creed, the Lord's Prayer, and the Ten Commandments, so families could participate in religious education. Parents were to inquire into their children's souls and discipleship week by week and were urged to withhold food from children who were less than zealous for the cause!

The Sinister Illusion

Luther's passion for instruction, his insistence that we (and not just the children) are almost desperate for instruction, was kindled by his awareness of the human predicament. For we are beleaguered by pride and bondage. However anxious Luther may have felt during the time he was outstripping even the most righteous in doing good and purifying his soul, what it all amounted to was pride, that sinister illusion that deceives us into thinking that we are spiritually capable, that our fate is determined by what we do and think, that we must fulfill the good potential within ourselves and are free to do so.

Almost embarrassingly, at least to the great thinkers of Renaissance Europe, Luther denied that we are free beings. We may feel free, but we are not. To personalize Luther's thought, I can decide to stand here or there, to do this or that—but all my supposedly free movements happen behind bars. I am very much trapped by sin, as if I have tumbled into a tangle of barbed wire from which I absolutely cannot extricate myself. I am not free to decide for or against God; rather, it is the unmerited grace of God that sets me free.

Luther's revolutionary discovery was "justification." The righteousness of God is not something up to which we must measure; rather, righteousness is a gift God freely bestows on us. What needs to be altered is not this or that behavior but rather the whole of human nature. Justification is waking up to realize that we have been set into a right relationship with God through no doing of our own. Our receiving of this free gift we call "faith."

But the gift is all gift, and it is unveiled in the cross of Christ. We can so easily take the cross for granted, featured as it is in fashion jewelry, in polished bronze at the altars of gilded churches, so utterly familiar that we miss its ugliness, the despicable offense that the brutal execution of a good man was and is. Why would God select such a horrendous, grotesque moment as the ultimate good gift to the world?

The Hiððenneʃʃ of God

Luther plumbed the depths of the hiddenness of God. Our mind can never fathom the fullness of God, so majestic and incomprehensible is the being of God. Reason cannot grasp God and can even mislead us about God. We know God not by what we see; empirical evidence is misleading. As David Steinmetz put it,

> The God who reveals himself in the pages of Holy Scripture is a God who works contrary to human expectation. The work of God is therefore not visible to sight, since everything the eye sees provides impressive grounds for distrusting the promises of God. The eye sees weakness not strength, folly not wisdom, humiliation not victory. Consequently Luther pits the ear against the eye. The Christian must hear by faith the promise which runs contrary to the empirical evidence his eye can assess and trust it.[21]

We know God by what we hear through the power of the word. And that word reveals a God who hides power in weakness.

In his famous *Table Talk*, Luther reflected often on the lowliness of Mary, that there was no room at the inn, observing that God became small for us in Christ, showing us the divine heart so that our hearts might be won. We do not need to ascend to God; God has descended to us. God came as a child, all gentleness, tenderness; no one need be afraid of a child. On Palm Sunday Jesus entered Jerusalem as a king. But he left all the pomp, castles, and gold to other kings. They enter cities on purebred stallions, accompanied by an impressive entourage; but Jesus was poor and wretched, riding on a donkey as a poor beggar-king.

God is most fully made known, not in some obvious victory, but in the apparently contradictory moment of the crucifixion. It is when God hides, when God is absent, and all is darkness and suffering that God is genuinely present, embracing our mortality and suffering. In the ninety-five theses, Luther stated, "God works by contraries so that a man feels himself to be lost in the very moment when he is on the point of being saved....Man must first cry out that there is no health in him....In this disturbance salvation begins. When a man believes himself to be utterly lost, light breaks."[22]

When Luther died in 1546, most presumed his reformation would end. But the movement was not his nor anyone else's. It depended on the power and creativity of God, and once the word of God was unleashed there was no reining it back in. Years earlier Luther had said that he could take no credit: "While I have been sleeping, or drinking Wittenburg beer with my friend Philip and with Amsdorf, it is the word that has done great things....I have done nothing; the word has done and achieved everything."[23]

SEIZED BY GRACE

The whole Reformation era was stunning. In school we learn about the heroism of the great scientists and explorers who redrew the map of what was possible for the species *homo sapiens*. But it was the Reformation, keeping pace with the intellectual Renaissance, while at the same time charting an alternate, almost countercultural, path for which we should be grateful. Charles Williams (one of the Inklings) noted how the year 1534 witnessed Luther's opening up of the scriptures to German eyes and ears; the extraordinary mission resolve of two Catholics, Ignatius Loyola and Francis Xavier; and the brilliant theological magnum opus of John Calvin.

The German Bible, the Jesuits, the *Institutes*—all in one
year. And Luther, Ignatius, Xavier, Calvin—the dates
of their births are important, but those other dates of
conversion are much more important. In that great age
of *Homo*, with its magnificences of scholarship, architec-
ture, art, exploration, war, its transient graces and ter-
rene glories, it pleased our Lord the Spirit violently to
convulse these souls with himself. Grace seized on
those strategic centres for its own campaign.[24]

Grace has indeed seized upon men and women over the
centuries, teachers who with wisdom and even courage
have explicated the truth of God to generations of learn-
ers. And the test of great teaching is not merely the dis-
section of truth. It can also be the ability and the willingness
to package that truth and deliver it to the people who need
it most. John Wesley and George Whitefield built schools
for orphans in England, believing that God would have
poor children to learn not just about God but also their
ABCs, arithmetic, and geography. Mary McLeod Bethune
in the first half of the twentieth century was a great teacher
who labored tirelessly to achieve fairness in the instruction of black Americans, pressing her concerns with
Franklin Delano Roosevelt in the White House.

As those black Americans grew up, they would need
an even more challenging kind of education. James
Lawson was handpicked by Martin Luther King Jr. to
teach nonviolent resistance to the vanguard of young black
seminarians who would revolutionize life in the South in
the sixties. Lawson's students were surprised by Lawson's
calm, measured speech, not fiery or titillating. Yet he
instilled in them a belief in their cause, in its rightness, and
in their ability to respond to hatred with love. David
Halberstam described him lucidly:

He spoke again and again of the awesome power of
action which was just in a land where the laws were
unjust. If they acted on conscience they would be immediately transformed; they would no longer be a handful
of unknown young students who had mounted a bizarre
and foolish challenge against powerful, entrenched
interests. This was his most crucial lesson: Ordinary
people who acted on conscience and took terrible risks
were no longer ordinary people. They were by their
very actions transformed. They would be heroes.[25]

Saints indeed are ordinary people who are transformed into
heroes by what they have been taught, by what they teach.

THE FOOLISHNESS OF GOD

We are surrounded by a great cloud of witnesses who continue to teach us about the God they knew intimately and
about ourselves—for the saints begin and end as ordinary
people, eager to know and live for God. The apostle Paul
did not pretend to be handsome or eloquent, but he grasped
intuitively the upside-down nature of the gospel—and his
detractors accused him of madness. In the world's eyes it
was madness—but in truth it was no less than the wisdom
of God (1 Cor. 1:18-31).

In the sixth grade I had a Sunday school teacher named
Floyd Busby. He seemed to be at least 147 years old. He
sported a flat top and spoke in a whiny voice. No one had
bothered to train him in hands-on, interactive instructional
techniques that were age-appropriate. *And why did he keep
coming back Sunday after Sunday?* We giggled and made fun
of him behind his back—or at least we stupidly presumed
to have cloaked our snickering.

But I remember Mr. Busby, and he changed my life.
One Sunday, while we were yawning and poking at one

another, he launched into a long, seemingly endless reading from his tattered Bible. We barely noticed the topic: the arrest of Jesus and how he was ridiculed, mocked, and beaten; how he bore a cross up a hill; how his feet and hands were nailed into the wood. Then to our surprise, there was a long silence. No more of that whiny voice. We looked up from our silly games to see why Mr. Busby had stopped. His head was hanging down—and we wondered if he had died. But he wasn't dead. He was crying—and this was in the 1960s, when men just didn't cry. Somehow we resisted the powerful temptation to laugh—but the temptation subsided, for somehow we knew we were in the presence of something holy. He fought back his sorrow and said to us, "Don't you boys see what they did to my Lord?"

I will never forget Mr. Busby's love for his Lord—and because of him I can say "our" Lord. Years later, having gained a little maturity and forever altered by the image of his plea, I tried to look him up and thank him for teaching me. But it was in vain. He was not to be found. He gave of himself all those years in teaching, probably with no compensation save the clamor of foolish, juvenile boys to get out of his room as quickly as possible. The foolishness of the gospel. But, like Thomas Aquinas, his fellow teacher and saint, Mr. Busby evidently sought no reward but Christ himself.

CHAPTER FIVE

PREACHERS

*It is easy to hear Christ, easy to praise the gospel,
easy to applaud the preacher: but to endure unto
the end, is peculiar to the sheep who hear the
Shepherd's voice.*[1]

—SAINT AUGUSTINE

Floyd Busby loved God. C. S. Lewis, who not only taught
but also preached from time to time about loving God, composed one of the greatest sermons in recorded history, delivering it at evensong at St. Mary's, Oxford, on June 8, 1941.
He begins "The Weight of Glory" by hazarding the guess
that good people in our century regard unselfishness as the
highest virtue, whereas the great Christians of old would
have ranked love as the zenith of the virtues. We have sub-
stituted a negative, assuming somehow that desires should
be denied, smothered, cooled. Then Lewis adds,

> If we consider the unblushing promises of reward and
> the staggering nature of the rewards promised in the
> Gospels, it would seem that Our Lord finds our desires
> not too strong, but too weak. We are half-hearted
> creatures, fooling about with drink and sex and ambition
> when infinite joy is offered us, like an ignorant child who
> wants to go on making mud pies in a slum because he
> cannot imagine what is meant by the offer of a holiday at
> the sea. We are far too easily pleased.[2]

Lewis is expounding that great verse from 2 Corinthians 4:17, where Paul tantalizes us: "For this slight momentary affliction is preparing us for an eternal weight of glory beyond all measure." Lewis's sermon continues by defining glory as "good report with God, acceptance by God." All our myriad cravings for this and that turn out to be rooted in a more primal seeking after God and the good God intends for us. Indeed, we are creatures made for glory, for togetherness with God, for even a share in the divine immortality. At the end Lewis unveils what this implies for us.

> The load, or weight, or burden of my neighbour's glory should be laid on my back, a load so heavy that only humility can carry it, and the backs of the proud will be broken. It is a serious thing to live in a society of possible gods and goddesses, to remember that the dullest and most uninteresting person you can talk to may one day be a creature which, if you say it now, you would be strongly tempted to worship, or else a horror and a corruption such as you now meet, if at all, only in a nightmare. All day long we are, in some degree, helping each other to one or other of these destinations....There are no *ordinary* people. You have never talked to a mere mortal....This does not mean that we are to be perpetually solemn. We must play. But our merriment must be of that kind (and it is, in fact, the merriest kind) which exists between people who have, from the outset, taken each other seriously.[3]

The Bible nowhere says that our desires are too weak or that we should not be perpetually solemn. But the sermon digs beneath Paul's words, dares to read between the lines, releases the energy of the gospel so that we absorb it directly into our faces, whispers the hope and challenge of the ages directly into our ears, pulls back the curtain, and ushers us into a friendship with God. This is what preaching does, and without preaching the curtain remains undrawn.

HOW ARE THEY TO HEAR?

The very existence of Christianity has from the start had a peculiar dependence on preachers. "How are they to hear without someone to proclaim him?" (Rom. 10:14). It is fascinating to contemplate what preachers have done. In just a dozen years Paul trekked over five thousand miles on foot and on creaky boats prone to shatter when the winds drove them helplessly onto the rocks, enduring floggings and imprisonments, planting and solidifying churches in four Roman provinces and on two continents, at Antioch on the Orontes, in Asia Minor (Turkey), throughout Greece. John Wesley was a preaching dynamo, trumpeting forth with eight hundred sermons in just one year in fields, streets, and coal mines. Francis Asbury rode a quarter of a million miles on horseback preaching in towns and out in the country up and down the eastern seaboard of America. Francis of Assisi even preached to a massive flock of birds, who stopped their chirping and silently heard him command them to be grateful for their feathers and for streams to drink from, for tall trees to nest in, and to sing praises to God all their days—at which point they lifted their wings, divided into four groups, and flew away, embodying the spread of the message of the cross to all the world.

Martin Luther King Jr. preached on the steps of the Lincoln Memorial on August 28, 1963, the body count on the Washington mall numbering in the hundreds of thousands; the extended congregation of us who have been transfixed by his "dream" numbers into the millions. And at a tiny Baptist church in Dover, Delaware, an aging, comparatively meek preacher we called "Brother Adams" proclaimed the word in such a way that I found myself walking up during the singing of "Just As I Am" and getting dunked beneath water in a glass-encased tank.

It is hard to measure excellence in preaching. What passes in one generation for stunning eloquence may bore the next. A style of preaching that is absolutely riveting to one batch of people will leave another crowd cold. Yet there are saints who still clamor for us to listen, preachers who spoke in such a way that they continue to speak.

GEORGE WHITEFIELD

The religious fervor of the American colonies was set ablaze by an Oxford-educated firebrand still in his twenties when he exploded on the scene as the most celebrated preacher of his day. George Whitefield (1714–1770), the "grand itinerant," preached in fields and near factories three times daily to raucous crowds. Some twenty thousand pressed onto Boston Common to hear him. His powerful voice trumpeted moving messages with stunning persuasiveness. David Garrick claimed Whitefield could melt a crowd just by pronouncing the word *Mesopotamia*. His preaching was great theater, sending many listeners into convulsions, about which he wrote an anxious letter to John Wesley. Even cynical old Benjamin Franklin noted that

> The multitudes of all sects and denominations that attended his sermons were enormous, and it was a matter of speculation to me, who was one of the number, to observe the extraordinary influence of his oratory on his hearers, and how they admir'd and respected him, notwithstanding his common abuse of them, by assuring

them they were naturally half beasts and half devils. It
was wonderful to see the change soon made in the manners of our inhabitants. From being thoughtless or indif-
ferent about religion, it seem'd as if all the world were
growing religious, so that one could not walk thro' the
town in an evening without hearing psalms sung in different families of every street.[4]

Franklin even admitted that he first came to hear Whitefield resolved in his mind to give nothing to the collection.
But after hearing the sermon, he emptied his pockets.

BILLY GRAHAM

America witnessed a great procession of pulpit giants;
Jonathan Edwards, Charles G. Finney, Dwight L. Moody,
and many other shining lights of the pulpit have dazzled
huge crowds. But for the sheer quantity of people reached,
pride of place goes to Billy Graham. Although his college
career began inauspiciously when he was pronounced a
failure and unlikely to amount to much by Dr. Bob Jones
Sr. (president of the college by the same name), Graham
was an overnight sensation on the preaching circuit, both
on the radio and in whirlwind crusades like "Youth for
Christ," the famous Los Angeles crusade of 1949, and a
grueling sixteen weeks of preaching in New York's
Madison Square Garden. The advent of loudspeaking sys-
tems and air travel enabled Graham to preach in person
on every continent to innumerable people (perhaps into
nine figures!) and to exponentially more people via the
technological wonder of television.

It is no small feat to be able with great simplicity and
clarity to proclaim the gospel to consistently huge crowds
across all cultural and national boundaries for six decades!

The impact on the lives of individuals, on families, on congregations, on communities staggers the mind and should be saluted with a chorus of praise.

All the more startling therefore is Graham's evident humility. He has aged like some vintage wine, growing not harder and more acidic (as did the golden-throated wonder of the prior generation, William Jennings Bryan) but warmer, wiser, gentler. While corruption has brought notoriety to huckster evangelists of Elmer Gantry's ilk, integrity has always been the hallmark of Graham's ministry. Early in his crusading life he met with Cliff Barrows and George Beverly Shea. They covenanted together, committing to financial accountability, honesty in publicity, determination to cooperate with local churches, and vowing never to meet alone with a woman.

Beginning with Harry Truman, every president has welcomed Graham into the White House—to the delight of many Christians in America. Predictably those most delighted by his visits were the presidents themselves, who basked in his popularity and no doubt chalked up points with the conservative religious community because of their friendship. And he got used a time or two by the powers that be. On the eve of the Gulf War, Graham was invited to spend the night in the Blue Room of the White House with President George Bush. Later Graham told the public that Bush "never asked me for any of my thoughts about it, nor did I volunteer them at the time (or since)."[5] His face and presence had to signal to many a blanket of blessing on the war. But preachers are called to speak even with heads of state, who need preachers too. In his autobiography, Graham recounted some fascinating exchanges with various presidents, including Dwight Eisenhower's tentative probing toward prayer and salvation.

Great Preaching

In Graham and Whitefield we can discover criteria for great preaching, which is not merely the clever crafting of a rhetorical gem. Rather the preacher needs to find where the people are. Whitefield at first had difficulty getting into some churches to preach, so ravenous were the crowds for his words. At Kingswood, a mining district near Bristol, he was told the colliers were infrequent in their attendance at holy worship. So he went to them and began to speak, and hundreds stopped their work enthralled. Day by day he preached, worrying some pundits who feared sky-rocketing prices for coal! Whitefield preached over eighteen thousand times—and the majority of his sermons were trumpeted in the fields, in barns, in courthouses and jails, standing in boats or straddling a horse, using windows and balconies as his pulpits. Graham packed stadiums and became a familiar face on prime time television.

Putting the gospel on television has not been without its perils though, as Graham was well aware. A great herd of preachers saw Graham on TV and took to the airwaves themselves—and a great disaster struck the church. A subtle danger lurks whenever religion becomes entertainment. Neil Postman has probingly inquired if television is at all an appropriate medium for preaching, concluding that "not everything is *televisible*."[6] Television is so much about the peddling of products, about what looks good. Stringent demands for changed lives just don't televise. When Christianity is pitched as amusing or as the best deal you ever came across, it is perverted into another kind of religion. The Christian faith, after all, is not necessarily pretty or sellable. Paul would not have looked good on TV. Jesus wound up on a cross, and a bloody execution seems far from what is handsomely packaged on slick televangelism shows. As Postman said of religion on TV: "Everything that makes religion an historic, profound and sacred human activity is stripped away; there is no ritual, no dogma, no tradition, no theology, and above all, no sense of spiritual transcendence. On these shows, the preacher is tops. God comes out as second banana."[7] Graham himself was "honored" with a star on Hollywood Boulevard!

This "star" appeal in preaching is a grave danger. Sinclair Lewis concocted the all too real character of Elmer Gantry, a huckster who knew how to look good and manipulate people. "He never said anything important, and he always said it sonorously."[8] He went into the ministry for all the wrong reasons: to please his mother, to get out of trouble, to rise socially, to flex some authority. He seemed to have a hard time staying converted. Even at the end, just as in midsermon he is resolving to be holy, to do those things he has urged on others,

> He turned to include the choir, and for the first time he saw that there was a new singer, a girl with charming ankles and lively eyes, with whom he would certainly have to become well acquainted. But the thought was so swift that it did not interrupt the paean of his prayer: "Let me count this day, Lord, as the beginning of a new and more vigorous life, as the beginning of a crusade for complete morality and the domination of the Christian church through all the land. Dear Lord, thy work is but begun! We shall yet make these United States a moral nation!"[9]

Television has created an embarrassment of top bananas, with the tube itself erected as the high altar in most homes.

Television has also narrowed our attention span, whetting our appetites for scrumptious little sound "bites," whereas the gospel requires thought, time, reflection, meditation, the searing of the soul, and a long painful process of change. Worst of all, television has those switches—the on/off switch and the other one with which we "surf" the channels. It's just too easy, if we don't like what we see, to switch it off or to scan about for a glitzier show. Jesus clearly would have been switched off before he got very far into the Sermon on the Mount.

And finally, television is a solitary experience. We all have been in a room talking with people—until the tube is turned on, after which time we stare blankly at it, and all interaction ceases. When preaching was put on television, it became easier to stay home and take in the sermon by yourself. You don't have to get dressed up or drive or park or be late for lunch. And you don't have to deal with those people who inevitably show up in the other pews. To Graham's great credit, his crusades, even when televised, pushed people hard to get involved in a local church.

FIRST EXPERIENCED BY DEEDS

Another criterion for great preaching would be a consistency between what the preacher says and how the preacher lives. Debauchery marked the youth of Whitefield; but after his conversion (in 1735) and ordination, his behavior was exemplary, to the point at times of being overbearing. Yet when he preached not merely about being born again but also about "fruits meet for repentance," he was not just blowing smoke. He built homes for the poor and schools for destitute children; he loved orphans and the homeless. Sojourner Truth, whom we shall consider in a moment, even after she became a free and famous woman, gave four years of her life caring for refugees living in shanties on Arlington Heights (the former Robert E. Lee estate) across the Potomac from Washington.

In more recent times Billy Graham insisted on integrated seating at his crusades; way back in 1953 he pulled down ropes that had been strung to separate white and black sections in Chattanooga, Tennessee. Then in 1973 he held evangelistic services for integrated crowds in Johannesburg and Durban in apartheid South Africa. His wife, Ruth, has been involved in work with felons and orphans. His son's work with Samaritan's Purse has been significant; Franklin Graham invaded Lebanon, not with incendiaries but with medicine and building supplies for hospitals. Wells and irrigation were brought to famine-ravaged Ethiopia. He has led mission work in Latin America, the Balkans, and throughout Asia.

The standard for the preacher was set by Saint Francis, as described by an early biographer Giovanni di Ceprano,

> Not with enticing words of human wisdom, but in the doctrine and virtue of the Holy Spirit he proclaimed the Kingdom of God with great confidence; as a true preacher....he never used flattering words and he despised all blandishments; what he preached to others in words, he had first experienced by deeds, so that he might speak the truth faithfully.[10]

A DISEMBODIED THEOLOGY

The saints remind us that great preaching connects to real life and changes real people. Preaching is not just about saving souls. Tony Campolo has poked some fun at superficial, merely emotional responses to preaching: You sing many stanzas of "Just As I Am." People come down the aisle, just as they are. Then they go out the door, just as they were. But the great cloud of witnesses through the history of God's church did not stay the way they were. The Christian life is about being different, setting out on an adventure of discipleship, holiness, service, and love — about which the great pulpit witnesses such as Billy Graham, George Whitefield, Francis of Assisi spoke with clarity and passion. Jesus did not come to town with a simple three-step message that invited people to get saved. His preaching focused on whom you invite to dinner, fathers and sons, turning the other cheek, how many barns you build, clothing the naked, picking up strangers by the side of the road. The miracle of preaching isn't just tabulating professions of faith but applying a word that can do surgery on those intractable diseases of lifestyle and habit, healing people so they might follow Jesus in the real world. The night before he was killed, Martin Luther King spoke at the Mason Temple, rallying support for the garbage workers of Memphis:

> It's alright to talk about "streets flowing with milk and honey," but God has commanded us to be concerned about the slums down here, and his children who can't eat three square meals a day. It's alright to talk about the new Jerusalem, but one day, God's preacher must talk about the New York, the new Atlanta, the new Philadelphia, the new Los Angeles, the new Memphis, Tennessee.[11]

This joining of the new Jerusalem with the real cities of our own day leads us to perhaps the most renowned preacher in the history of Christendom: John Chrysostom.

JOHN CHRYSOSTOM

Chrysostom was not his real name but a reverential nickname meaning "golden-mouthed." John was born in

Antioch around 349. His family was well-off, living in a
large villa with mosaic-laden floors. As a young man he
lived for four years in a hermitage with other monks, devot-
ing his day to silent meditation on the scriptures. Then he
spent two years absolutely alone in a cave, enduring the
assaults of loneliness and climate and disease with no assis-
tance save the divine, but his calling was back in Antioch,
in the life of the world.

Chrysostom was short, with an unusually large head,
and his body was pitiful, ravaged by years of fasting and
exposure to the elements. Between his notably big ears
and above a scraggly beard were deeply set, piercing eyes.
But his voice was penetrating. His grasp of the Bible was
astonishing, and he knew how to urge people to hear and
practice its words. So spectacular were his gifts that while
still in his thirties, he was asked by his bishop, Flavian, to
preach in the city's largest and most splendid pulpit, the
renowned octagonal Golden Church.

Citizens could not hear him often enough, greeting his
brilliant expositions of scripture with thunderous applause,
despite his urging them to be silent. With a captivating
blend of picturesque imagery and stylistic charisma, he
held even pagans spellbound. He preached extempora-
neously. Stenographers scrambled to capture his stunning
eloquence on paper—and discovered that his seemingly
free-wheeling sermons were structural masterpieces. He
was superbly trained in oratory, but he could be earthy,
as he understood the power of an image. Hearts were
touched, even inflamed. Injuries were common as throngs
surged forward just to get close.

Chrysostom's words were far from soothing. Those
being baptized were urged to dazzle others by their holy
behavior. They should particularly avoid horse races and

the world →

the theater. In one brilliant sermon, he noted his flock's enthusiasm at the hippodrome; they apparently felt more passionately about a race than about the sacrifice of Christ on the cross. He observed that in the theater men gawked at beautiful women, whose seductive songs and gestures stayed with the men long after they had returned home. Chrysostom diagnosed the psychology of theater-going and saw its harmful effects on family life, which seemed boring by comparison. Chrysostom had no tolerance for the lukewarm.

Preaching to the Empress

After a dozen years in Antioch, he was virtually abducted and installed as bishop in the capital of the eastern empire, Constantinople. There he filled the pulpit of the Great Church, the Hagia Sophia, and found himself pastor to the emperor and the empress. Swiftly he began to offend, delivering the jolting surprise that he intended to live out what he preached, even in the halls of privilege. Instead of spending extravagantly as had his predecessors, Bishop John Chrysostom lived modestly and took no interest in attending sumptuous feasts and parties. He used the money instead to build a hospital for lepers, which infuriated the well-heeled Christians of the city who delighted in great dinners and receptions in the gilded halls of Hagia Sophia.

In both Antioch and Constantinople, two of the largest cities in the world, Chrysostom openly addressed the nagging, universal urban woes of poverty. He was the champion of the poor, which no one minded until he made a connection between their plight and the affluence of the rich, whose luxurious lifestyle proved they had no compassion for the poor. Just as Mother Teresa in our century focused on seeing Christ in the poor, Chrysostom

could preach like this: "You would throw away your very
souls for your pantomime dancers, but to Christ when he
is starving you would not hand over the smallest piece of
money. If you do give a few pence, it is as if you had given
away your entire fortune."[12]

Chrysostom's challenge was twofold: how to proclaim
the gospel accurately, given its repeated summons to alleviate poverty; and how to have church, when some Christians were rich and others were destitute.

Chrysostom tirelessly argued that riches are not evil,
but they are intended by God for sharing. He lamented
the use of "those chilly words 'mine' and 'yours.'"[13] Christians may use what money is necessary; but all that is above
mere necessity is a trust, placed in our hands for sharing.
Citizens of Antioch and Constantinople were just as capable as you and I of heightening the level of necessity to
absurd levels. He unmasked their greed:

> You plunder and are grasping, not impelled to it by
> poverty, without any hunger to necessitate you, but that
> your horse's bridle may be spattered over with gold
> enough, or the ceiling of your house, or the capitals of
> your pillars. And what hell is there that this conduct
> would not deserve, when it is a brother, and one
> that...has been so highly honored by the Lord, whom
> you, in order that you may deck out stones, and
> floors,...are casting into countless calamities? And your
> dog is well attended too, while man, or rather Christ, for
> the sake of the hound,...is straitened in extreme hunger.
> What can be worse than such confusion? What more
> grievous than such lawlessness as this? What streams of
> fire will be enough for such a soul? He that was made in
> the image of God stands in unseemly plight, through thy
> inhumanity; but the faces of the mules that draw thy
> wife glisten with gold in abundance.[14]

A Christian closet should not be stuffed with the finest fabrics while others created in God's image are left naked and shivering in the streets. Like Francis of Assisi, Chrysostom wanted a new life, not just for the poor but also for the rich; he saw the insidious, paralyzing effects wealth has on the soul. "Wealth that is locked up and buried is fiercer than a lion and causes great fright. But if you bring it out and distribute it among the poor, the fierce beast becomes a lamb."[15]

The idolatry of wealth can seize not just the rich but also the poor; Chrysostom warned even the poor against the perils of believing that money is the great healer and bringer of life and hope. In place of gold, carpets, and teams of servants, a person's true glory resides in gentleness, faith, humility, and generosity.

The Deserving Poor

To have church, there must be sharing, a redistribution of goods. Andrew Carnegie taught us what we Americans typically believe about stewardship. This great philanthropist, viewed by others as a robber baron, believed that capitalism is good and that you have every right to accumulate wealth. It is good to engage in some philanthropy—and the recipients should be what Carnegie called "the deserving poor." Our estimation of who is deserving and who isn't often cripples our giving. Chrysostom settled this issue:

> "But he fakes all that weakness and trembling," you tell me. And, saying so, you do not fear that a bolt of lightning will strike you from heaven?...You who fatten yourselves and enjoy your ease, you who drink well into the night, and then cover yourselves with soft blankets,...you dare demand a strict account from the needy who is little more than a corpse, and you fear not the account you will have to render before the court of Christ, terrible and frightful? If the poor fake, it is out of

need that they fake, for it is your merciless inhumanity and your cruelty that forces them to do so.... We point our finger at the idleness of the poor, and yet we ourselves often work at things that are worse than idleness.... You who often spend the day in the theatres and in merryments, you who gossip about the whole world, think that you are not idle. And then you look at someone who spends the entire day asking and begging, in tears and suffering, and you dare ask for an account![16]

For Chrysostom, it is clearly better to give to some who are unworthy than to risk failing to give to some in genuine need. And he trusted even the evangelistic appeal of compassion and sharing. He preached repeatedly and forcefully on the early chapters of Acts, urging his listeners to share their wealth communally, claiming that if they did hold all things in common, they would soon convert the whole world without any need of miracles at all.

The miracle is that he was allowed to preach in such a way as long as he did. He contrasted the golden jewelry worn by wealthy women, and even the empress Eudoxia herself, with the chains that shackled Paul in prison. In a demonstration of utter fearlessness, Chrysostom compared the empress to Jezebel—and that was perhaps the final straw. So offended was Eudoxia that she expelled him from the city. Receiving this news, the populace of the city rioted and, in all the confusion, managed to set the church ablaze. The most fantastic preacher in history, exiled to Armenia, died in seeming disgrace at age fifty-eight.

The test of preaching, we may then conclude, is complex. Is it faithful to God's word and not just to those convenient, pleasing segments? Does preaching have an impact on people, and not just on the final fate of their souls? Does it dare to "meddle"? Or, to shift perspective: Are we the kind of people who are willing to be exposed and to have our lives altered? Chrysostom reminded his listeners to repeat his words to their families, to discuss them at mealtime, "thereby transforming their homes into churches, indeed into heaven itself."[17]

Fifteen hundred years later, another preacher transformed home life into heaven itself—as perhaps only a mother could.

Archive Photos

SOJOURNER TRUTH

In an era of great orators, such as Charles Grandison Finney, Abraham Lincoln, Frederick Douglass, and Charles Haddon Spurgeon, no one in the nineteenth century could leave listeners as thunderstruck as Sojourner Truth. Named Isabella when she was born a slave in Ulster County, New York, she spent her youth at hard labor, punctuated with heavy doses of physical and sexual abuse. In 1826, toting her infant Sophia, she ran away and fortunately had her freedom purchased for twenty dollars by the Van Wagenens, an abolitionist family she had never even met.

As a free woman Truth bounced around among religious groups, taking turns at being Methodist, A.M.E. Zion, and Pentecostal. She was supportive of groups like the Millerites, who were convinced Christ would return during 1843. She was buried in a Presbyterian cemetery. Through it all, no matter whether she had been treated with brutality as a slave or with accolades as a preacher, she came to a keen awareness that Jesus was her friend and that the Spirit was leading her.

It was discovered during camp meetings that she could speak, that even the educated and wealthy (although she never learned to read) couldn't get enough of her. Standing five feet, eleven inches tall, blessed with an astonishing voice and clever wit, she held audiences in thrall as she wrought hundreds of conversions. Her lasting fame is linked to the way she spoke out against slavery and in favor of women's suffrage and temperance. The name she invented for herself spoke volumes: A sojourner is someone who is never totally at home, who is on a journey to some destination, and truth was her passion in a culture not always ready to hear truth.

Blending words, song, and humor, deploying winks and hilarious gestures, Truth preached sermons that were unforgettable. Dealing with Matthew 25:31-46, she began, "Well, there are two congregations on this ground. It is written that there shall be a separation, and the sheep shall be separated from the goats. The other preachers have the sheep, I have the goats. And I have a few sheep among my goats, but they are very ragged."[18]

Arn't I a Woman?

At one point she even tore open her dress and exposed her breast during a sermon before a hostile crowd. But she was not shamed; they were. The sight was not unfamiliar in those days: At slave auctions, women were undressed and exhibited. As a slave she had been bought and sold. She had served as a wet-nurse, and now she forced the crowd to see that the one being sold and used was a child of God. In another sermon, or perhaps in a cleaned-up version of the same sermon, she bared her arm and asked, "Arn't I a woman? Look at me. Look at my arm."[19] And she proceeded to tell how she had plowed and planted, how she had endured lashings, and how she had carried many children. To a minister who interrupted her, she pointedly inquired, "Where did your Christ come from?"[20]

Truth deftly chose passages from the Bible that could not easily be eluded. The book of Esther was a favorite, harsh as it could be both on prejudice and male dominance. "The women are coming up blessed by God and a few of the men are coming up with them. But man is in a tight place, the poor slave is on him, woman is coming on him, and he is surely between a hawk and a buzzard."[21]

She was direct in exposing human sin — but was always hopeful. As she denounced slavery, she offered forgiveness for slaveholders. As she spoke alongside Elizabeth Cady Stanton and Lucretia Mott, she even dared to suggest that women were not entirely innocent victims: "I can't read, but I can hear. I have heard the bible and have learned that Eve caused man to sin. Well if woman upset the world, do give her a chance to set it right side up again."[22]

Truth's fame skyrocketed after Harriet Beecher Stowe stumbled upon her and wrote a popular account of her life. Truth met Presidents Lincoln, Johnson, and Grant. Yet she always spoke bluntly. Once she was on the front row of an audience being regaled by the fiery oratory of the abolitionist Frederick Douglass. He had no faith that blacks would ever be treated decently by whites; therefore, blacks must seize their freedom by force of arms: "It must come to blood; they must fight for themselves, and redeem themselves, or it would never be done." Sojourner Truth, in her deep, resonant voice, upbraided him: "Frederick, *is God dead?*"[23] Stowe said, "The effect was perfectly electrical, and thrilled through the whole house, changing as by a flash the whole feeling of the audience. Not another word she said or needed to say; it was enough." Douglass himself reminisced that "we were all for a moment brought to a stand-still, just as we should have been if someone had thrown a brick through the window."[24]

When Truth died in 1883, she guessed she was 105 years old. Her last words were a brief but eloquent sermon: "Be a follower of the Lord Jesus."

MARTIN NIEMÖLLER

A native of Westphalia, Martin Niemöller was born on January 14, 1892. His exploits aboard a World War I U-boat earned him the Iron Cross. In 1917 he even fired unsuccessfully at a French steamer bearing a passenger named Albert Schweitzer! But after the war, he took up his father's profession and in 1924 was ordained a Lutheran pastor.

When Hitler emerged as chancellor in 1933, Niemöller was optimistic and hopeful, as were most Germans. But he was one of the first to see the evil lurking beneath the veneer of patriotism. Alongside Karl Barth, he organized resistance to the regime and began to speak out vehemently against Nazi excesses. Summoned to the Führer's office, Niemöller spoke boldly to Hitler's face when many had cowered in fright: "The responsibility for our German nation has been laid upon our souls and conscience by no earthly authority but by God himself, and no earthly authority can take away this responsibility from our hearts, not even you."[25] Hitler threw a tantrum, and Niemöller left a marked man.

Police spied on his worship services. But Niemöller's

courage in the pulpit was unrelenting, choosing biblical texts such as "We must obey God rather than men" and "You are the salt of the earth," urging the church not to lose its savor, not to make a German church out of Christ's church. His final sermons were collected in a volume with the daring title *God Is My Führer*. Subjected to harassment, searches, and finally arrest by the Gestapo, Niemöller was convicted in a mock trial and spent eight years in various prisons, enduring torture and solitary confinement.

His faith was like salt, preserving and flavoring life for his fellow prisoners. After miraculously surviving the war, he returned to preaching, continuing to speak out against the Cold War, nuclear proliferation, and economic and racial injustice. As the journal *Die Welt* described him, "Niemöller has made friends and many enemies but he leaves nobody cold."[26]

THE FRUITFULNESS OF PREACHING

The preaching saints in our cloud of witnesses remind us that there is a "timeliness" to the word of God. In chapter 1 we heard Martin Luther say that the loyalty of the soldier is proved where the battle rages, on the battlefield where the world and devil are at that moment attacking. We have surveyed many battlefields: wretched poverty in Constantinople and Kingswood, slavery and racism in the South, fascism and genocide in Europe, a lost world that has never heard of Christ. Thanks be to God, the loyalty of God's soldiers—Wesley, Chrysostom, Truth, Niemöller, Graham, Whitefield, King, and Paul—has been proved.

What all these great soldiers of the pulpit would say is that, even though they go and speak to the pinnacle of their abilities, the fruitfulness of the preached word rests entirely in God's hands. As we saw in the last chapter, Martin Luther, himself one of the most important preachers in history, knew that when the word is proclaimed and heard, all the credit goes to God, who was working while Luther was sleeping and drinking Wittenburg beer.

As Christians, it is the word from this God for which we must listen, getting beyond the façade of the preacher's personality or oratorical skills. We also have learned that we are all called, not just to be hearers of the word, but also doers of the word. When God speaks, lives are changed: We must bare our souls and let that word do its work and have its way with us.

The word of God leaves nobody cold. The truly spoken word will not often be popular. Bricks fly through windows. Churches are set ablaze. Whitefield was pelted with eggs. Vernon Johns, who preceded Martin Luther King Jr. in the Dexter Avenue Baptist pulpit in Montgomery, was hauled off to jail for putting his sermon title ("Segregation After Death") on the church bulletin board facing the sidewalk.

Three years before anyone had ever heard of Rosa Parks, Johns boarded a Montgomery bus, only to have the driver "accidentally" drop the preacher's money to the floor. "Boy!" the driver barked, "get down and pick up that dime." As Johns with great dignity turned to disembark, he spoke to church members seated on the bus: "Come on, children, let's get off this bus." No one budged. Later a woman upbraided him for his behavior, which led Johns to complain to his friend Ralph Abernathy, "Even God can't free people who behave like that."[27] The sermon may be pronounced at any place, at any time, and its effectiveness depends on people hearing but even more on their acting, embodying the proclaimed word in changed lives.

CHAPTER SIX

Sĩngers

*The world belongs primarily to the dead, and we
only rent it from them for a little while. They
created it, they wrote its literature and its songs,
and they are deeply invested in how children are
treated, because the children are the ones who will
keep it going. The idea that each of us has the
right to change everything is a deep insult to
them.*[1]

—Robert Bly

(handwritten: Those who went before us — we owe deep gratitude)

In the earliest years of Israel's history with God, before
people got busy writing history as we think of it, the faithful sang songs, some akin to what we might regard as bal-
lads, all of them hymns of praise. In some profound way,
what God is about cannot be captured by mere prose; our
language is too "prosaic" for God. God is somehow higher,
grander, deeper, requiring specialized language, poetic
devices and meter, and not just spoken but also sung. From
what we know about the psalms, these songs were accompanied not just by instruments but by human movement,
by dance. So great is this God that every fiber of our being
must be exploited in our attempts to express anything
about such a God.

THE HEARTS OF ALL THE SAINTS

Thomas Merton prized the Psalms because, in them, "we drink divine praise at its pure and stainless source, in all its primitive sincerity and perfection. We return to the youthful strength and directness with which the ancient psalmists voiced their adoration of the God of Israel...for the Psalms are the songs of men who knew who God was."[2]

In a day when praise is cheap, when a torrent of superlatives drowns out all meaningful adulation of God, we need to strain to see the faces of psalmists, to hear their songs and cries, to be swept up in their chorus of praise to the God they knew more intimately than we. As Martin Luther put it,

Martin Luther

A human heart is like a ship on a wild sea, driven by the storm winds from the four corners of the world. Here it is struck with fear and worry about impending disaster; there comes grief and sadness because of present evil. Here breathes a breeze of hope and of anticipated happiness; there blows security and joy in present blessings. These storm winds teach us to speak with earnestness, to open the heart and pour out what lies at the bottom of it....What is the greatest thing in the Psalter but this earnest speaking amid these storm winds of every kind? Where does one find finer words of joy than in the psalms of praise and thanksgiving? There you look into the hearts of all the saints, as into fair and pleasant gardens, yes, as into heaven itself.[3]

Imagine someone standing near a thunderous waterfall created by the melting snows of Mount Hermon, watching a desperate deer finally able to quench his thirst, sensing in that moment a roaring chaos within, a profound thirst for God:

> As a deer longs for flowing streams,
>   so my soul longs for you, O God.
> . . . .
> My soul is cast down within me;
>   therefore I remember you
> from the land of Jordan and of Hermon....
> Deep calls to deep
>   at the thunder of your cataracts. (Ps. 42:1, 6-7)

Stand next to the singer who lies on the grass in a field at night, gazing into skies that are darker (and whose stars therefore are brighter) than ours, stunned by the majestic expanse, awed by its creator:

> When I look at your heavens, the work of your fingers,
>   the moon and the stars that you have established;
> what are human beings that you are mindful of them,
>   mortals that you care for them?
> Yet you have made them a little lower than God. (Ps. 8:3-5a)

Can you see the anguished face of the one whose trauma can only be described with words like these?

> Be gracious to me, O Lord, for I am languishing;
>   O Lord, heal me, for my bones are shaking
>   with terror.
> . . . .

I am weary with my moaning;
every night I flood my bed with tears. (Ps. 6:2, 6)

Widen your gaze and look at the throng of pilgrims who have braved the elements in great caravans, crowding around the hill of Mount Zion. The shofar blares, smoke curls heavenward; and as the ark of the covenant is hoisted aloft at the head of a processional into the temple precincts, the people cry out in deafening unison:

The Lord, the Most High, is awesome,
a great king over all the earth. (Ps. 47:2)

Their worship is enthusiastic, downright noisy:

Clap your hands, all you peoples;
shout to God with loud songs of joy.
. . . .
God has gone up with a shout,
the Lord with the sound of a trumpet.
Sing praises to God, sing praises. (Ps. 47:1, 5-6)

Then comes that even more deafening moment of stillness:

Be still, and know that I am God! (Ps. 46:10)

Dare you smell the burning fat and oozing blood of lambs burnt on the altar, while words of faith are sung:

I will offer to you burnt offerings of fatlings,
with the smoke of the sacrifice of rams;
. . . .
Come and hear, all you who fear God,
And I will tell what he has done for me. (Ps. 66:15-16)

Can you even listen closely enough to that last scream, that outburst of utter despair from the lips of Jesus, himself now the sacrificial lamb on a dark Friday in the year 30?

"My God, my God, why have you forsaken me?"
(Ps. 22:1; Mark 15:34)

And yet hidden beneath Jesus' desperation, can you hear his plea—or even an undergirding of the profoundest faith and trust? Look long into the pained but hopeful eyes of that most eloquent psalmist who suffered much but still with amazing confidence prayed:

> Whom have I in heaven but you?
>> And there is nothing on earth that I desire
>> other than you.
> My flesh and my heart may fail,
>> but God is the strength of my heart and
>> my portion forever.
> Indeed, those who are far from you will perish;
>> you put an end to those who are false to you.
> But for me it is good to be near God;
>> I have made the Lord God my refuge,
>> to tell of all your works. (Ps. 73:25-28)

Jesus prayed the psalms. These words to God have become for us the word of God, and they can indeed school us in the ways of prayer.

A GROWING CHORUS

We also can see tantalizing glimpses of hymns sung by the earliest Christians. They sang psalms, of course. When Paul wrote to the Philippians, he reminded them of a hymn they had sung in praise of Christ,

> who, though he was in the form of God,
> did not regard equality with God as something
>> to be exploited,
> but emptied himself, taking the form of a slave,
> being born in human likeness.
> And being found in human form,
> he humbled himself and became obedient to the point
>> of death —
> even death on a cross. (Phil. 2:6-8)

Strands of other hymns are scattered here and there (for example, 1 Tim. 3:16). But the book that cannot be read without hearing a mighty heavenly chorus in the background is Revelation. Throbbing behind, beneath, and above the kaleidoscopic images of John's vision into the heavens is the score of a choir that never flags in its zeal to sing praise to the Lamb of God. The creatures hovering about the throne sing day and night, without ceasing:

> Holy, holy, holy
> the Lord God the Almighty,
>   who was and is and is to come. (4:8)

Joined by the elders who cast their crowns before the throne, they sing a new song:

> You are worthy to take the scroll
>   and to open its seals,
> for you were slaughtered and by your blood
>   you ransomed for God
>   saints from every tribe and language and people
>   and nation. (5:9)

The crowd swells by myriads of myriads,

> Worthy is the Lamb that was slaughtered
> to receive power and wealth and wisdom and might.
> (5:12)

before all creatures in the universe unite in song,

> To the one seated on the throne and to the Lamb
>   be blessing and honor and glory and might
> forever and ever! (5:13)

The Lamb is praised for the gift of that great hope when

> they will hunger no more, and thirst no more;...

and God will wipe away every tear from their eyes.
(7:16-17)

No small witness to a profound faith, this kind of singing.
For not only does John overhear and transcribe this chorus from a penal colony on the island of Patmos; all
Christians, still toddlers in their faith, are looking over their
shoulders in fear as news of sporadic persecution and
harassment begins to spread. Despotic emperors, first Nero
and then Domitian, back up with executions their demands
literally to be worshiped. We will explore the dilemma of
Christians who face martyrdom in chapter 8, but for now
we have to notice—and be awed by the way believers stand
up and sing in the teeth of evil, answering their tormen-
tors with doxology instead of denial.

In Revelation the angels, archangels, saints, and the
heavenly host never weary of song. As the new Jerusalem
is about to appear, John "heard what seemed to be the
voice of a great multitude, like the sound of many waters
and like the sound of mighty thunderpeals, crying out,

"Hallelujah!
For the Lord our God the Almighty reigns
Let us rejoice and exult and give him the glory,
for the marriage of the Lamb has come,
    and his bride has made herself ready." (19:6-7)

Somehow it is of the essence of our eternal destiny to be
in a choir, to "lift every voice and sing," "lost in wonder,
love, and praise." Praise is not merely some noble endeavor
for today but an anticipation of our eternal vocation. From
the island of Patmos is therefore whispered a hint that
when we sing praise to God, we are swept up into something greater than ourselves, greater than this earth, into
something cosmic in its reach.

DANTE ALIGHIERI

The cosmic yet deeply personal scope of the drama of salvation was captured by the greatest of all medieval poets Dante Alighieri. He was born into a noble family in Florence in 1265, but economic misfortune had left them nearly destitute. While befriending troubadours in his youth, he taught himself to write verse and produced love poetry, about which he was embarrassed later in life. After a rise to political prominence as a leader of the Guelf party, he was expelled from the city on bogus charges at age thirty-six, spending the rest of his days as an exile in Ravenna.

Just months before his death in 1321, Dante completed an epic poem called *Commedia (Comedy)*. Its title derived from the words *comus* and *oda*, "a rustic song." Instead of using high church Latin, Dante wrote in the Italian "rustic" vernacular. And while a tragedy may begin happily and conclude in sorrow, a comedy always has a happy ending. This poem is in some ways the spiritual biography of every person, while not lacking in the poet's own experiences. Dante's *Comedy* falls into three massive sections: Inferno (or Hell), Purgatory, and only then Paradise. The poem begins where we all find ourselves:

> Midway along the journey of our life
> I woke to find myself in a dark wood,
> for I had wandered off from the straight path.[4]

Dante, who is every pilgrim, tries to scale a mountain to get out of the dark wood, but beasts representing sin block the way. His appointed guide Virgil (who represents human understanding), informs him that the only route to get to the mountain goes through Hell itself; to go up one must first go down and plumb the depths of life apart from God. The foreboding sign at Hell's entrance reads,

"Abandon every hope, all you who enter"[5]; and as they traverse the complex regions of the netherworld, they observe multifarious sinners to whom harsh punishment is being meted out.

The only exit from Hell, which is cold as ice, is by climbing across the body of Lucifer himself, the stony frigidity of pride. Only after looking evil straight in the eye can they begin the ascent toward hope.

> We climbed, he first and I behind, until,
>   through a small round opening ahead of us
> I saw the lovely things the heavens hold,
>   and we came out to see once more the stars.[6]

The mountain of purgatory features terrible cliffs and treacherous ledges—a zone of repentance and refining for the soul. The sense of being homesick is a sign both of being far from God and of longing for and progressing toward God. Virgil can no longer be Dante's guide; human reason can only carry one so far. Beatrice, a beautiful woman Dante had adored before and after her premature death in 1290, takes over, representing as she does divine revelation.

After much travail, Dante and Beatrice come to paradise. Dante fears some great separation of souls at such an ethereal height. But Beatrice explains:

> Not the most Godlike of the Seraphim,
> not Moses, Samuel, whichever John
> you choose—I tell you—not Mary herself
>   has been assigned to any other heaven
>   than that of these shades you have just seen here,
>   and each one's bliss is equally eternal;
>   all lend their beauty to the Highest Sphere,
>   sharing one same sweet life to the degree
>   that they feel the eternal breath of God.[7]

It is this proximity to God, being at home with God, that is the goal of all their striving, the zenith of the soul's quest. The grand epic ends as Dante gazes into God's light and discovers he is home, that he belongs.

> My eyes were totally absorbed in It.
> As the geometer who tries so hard
> to square the circle, but cannot discover,
>   think as he may, the principle involved,
>   so did I strive with this new mystery:
>   I yearned to know how could our image fit
> into that circle, how could it conform;
> but my own wings could not take me so high —
> then a great flash of understanding struck
>   my mind, and suddenly its wish was granted.
>   At this point power failed high fantasy
> but, like a wheel in perfect balance turning,
> I felt my will and my desire impelled
> by the Love that moves the sun and the other
>   stars.[8]

A CLOUD OF POETS

Dante was not the only troubadour-turned-saintly poet. Francis of Assisi, whose humble face appears in virtually every chapter of this book, began his presaintly life as a troubadour. After he became poor for the sake of Christ, the poet inside him extolled his creator. Francis's *The Canticle of Creatures* conducts a great chorus of the elements of earth and sky, sun, moon, stars and wind, and animals and plants, all of them brothers and sisters, siblings in the great family of God the Father, in praise and adoration:

> Most high, all-powerful, all good, Lord!
>   All praise is yours, all glory, all honour
>   And all blessing.
> To you alone, Most High, do they belong.

> No mortal lips are worthy
> to pronounce your name.
> All praise be yours, my Lord, through all
> that you have made.[9]

The spiritual life of the church has always been nourished by great poetry. John Donne penned one of his most famous sonnets as a prayer:

> Batter my heart, three-person'd God, for you
> As yet but knock, breathe, shine, and seek to mend
> ....
> Take me to you, imprison me, for I
> Except you enthrall me, never shall be free,
> Nor ever chaste, except you ravish me.

John Milton, composer of the familiar line, "They also serve who only stand and wait," plumbed the depths of the human predicament and hope in his twin works, *Paradise Lost* and *Paradise Regained*. William Blake put his visionary experiences onto paper in his provocative drawings such as "The Ancient of Days" and in grand poetry ("And we are put on earth a little space, that we may learn to bear the beams of love"). Francis Thompson, after nearly squandering his talent and life, told his and our story in "The Hound of Heaven":

> I fled Him, down the nights and down the days,
> I fled Him, down the arches of the years
> I fled Him, down the labyrinthine ways
> of my own mind; and in the mist of tears
> I hid from Him, and under running laughter.

But God, the "hound of heaven," pursued him "with unperturbed pace."

Gerard Manley Hopkins perceived that "the world is charged with the grandeur of God," and James Weldon

Johnson devised a collection of poetic sermons (in *God's Trombones*), including "Go down, Death." Indeed, a great cloud of witnesses have answered Paul Gerhardt's question, "What language shall I borrow to thank thee, dearest friend?" Poets and hymn writers surely rank as saints; their deeds were their words and songs.

MUSIC AND REFORM

These great poets and singers do not only serve as guides, like Virgil and Beatrice, showing us the way up toward God. They also ferry God down, stretching the imagination, enabling the divine to become reality on earth and in the church. Music was certainly pivotal in the sixteenth-century Reformation. Luther knew music's power to heal and encourage. For him, there was nothing like a good hymn to drive away the devil! Luther had promoted the usage of hymns in the vernacular and wrote a few himself, most famously "A Mighty Fortress Is Our God," written at a time of profound depression in his own life. Hear this earthy saint:

> Music is a fair and lovely gift of God which has often wakened and moved me to the joy of preaching....I have no use for cranks who despise music, because it is a gift of God. Music drives away the devil and makes people gay; they forget thereby all wrath, unchastity, arrogance and the like. Next after theology I give to music the highest place and the greatest honor....This precious gift has been bestowed on men alone to remind them that they are created to praise and magnify the Lord. But when natural music is sharpened and polished by art, then one begins to see with amazement the great and perfect wisdom of God in his wonderful work of music, where one voice takes a

delightful

simple part and around it sing three, four, or five other
voices, leaping, springing round about, marvelously
gracing the simple part, like a square dance in heaven
with friendly bows, embracings, and hearty swinging of
the partners. [One] who does not find this an
inexpressible miracle of the Lord is truly a clod.[10]

Under Luther's direction, singing was no longer reserved
for a choir or a cantor, but the entire congregation sang
often in the service.

CHARLES WESLEY

The role of music and singing in the reformation of church
life continued apace in eighteenth-century England, the
era that bequeathed to us the prolific Charles Wesley. For
long stretches, he averaged composing one hymn per day,
totaling at least 6,500 before his death in 1788. Born in
1707, he was second youngest of Samuel and Susanna's
nineteen children. His father wrote a few hymns while serving at Epworth. Charles was educated at Oxford. Although
his father was a priest, Charles inherited his spirituality
from his mother. Among her prayers were these words:

> Help me, Lord, to remember that religion is not to be
> confined to the church, or closet, nor exercised only in
> prayer and meditation, but that everywhere I am in thy
> presence. So may my every word and action have a
> moral content....May all the happenings of my life
> prove useful and beneficial to me. May all things
> instruct me and afford me an opportunity of exercising
> some virtue and daily learning and growing toward
> Thy likeness....Amen.[11]

Like his intrepid brother John, Charles preached frequently and traveled widely. He knew the joys of life (a

marriage of thirty-eight years) and its sorrows (the death of five of his eight children in infancy).

His hymns were "not the product of a lively imagination…nor were they the fruit of hard mental toil. They were the spontaneous effusions of his heart."[12] From that heart we have learned to think of Jesus as "lover of my soul," to harken to "the herald angels" at Christmas, to long to have the absurdly high number of "a thousand tongues to sing my great redeemer's praise."

This latter hymn stands as the first in virtually every collection of Methodist hymns. On the day of Pentecost in 1738, Charles attended a Moravian service and at midnight gave his life to Christ—less than a week before his brother John's more famous Aldersgate experience of the "heart strangely warmed." "O for a Thousand Tongues to Sing" was written to commemorate that conversion. Stretching to eighteen stanzas, the image wasn't entirely original; Charles's mentor, Peter Böhler, had written, "Had I a thousand tongues, I would praise him with them all!"

Charles Wesley's goal was "to arouse sinners, encourage saints, and to educate all in the mysteries of the Christian faith."[13] He understood that hymns were not just inspirational but also educational. He used contemporary folk tunes, melodies from Italian opera, as well as oratorio (especially favoring Handel). It was in part by the singing of hymns that the early Methodists learned theology, were reshaped as people of faith, and were catapulted into the streets in mission. The Wesleyan revival in Britain and in America changed the face of an entire culture, a culture whose ugliest feature was slavery.

JOHN NEWTON

Music changed the lives of white slaveholders. John Newton was born in 1725 in London and became a seaman noted for his vulgarity and debauchery. Newton's startling conversion in 1748, the preaching of George Whitefield, and the ministry of John Wesley led to the composition of perhaps the most popular hymn ever written, "Amazing Grace." His tombstone in Olney, England, bears this duly famous epitaph: "John Newton, clerk, once an infidel and libertine, a servant of slavers in Africa, was by the rich mercy of our Lord and Saviour, Jesus Christ, preserved, restored, pardoned, and appointed to preach the faith he had long labored to destroy."

Such words etched in granite could only stand as a challenge to a man like William Wilberforce, whose life was changed by having Newton as his pastor. On May 12, 1789, Wilberforce stood in the House of Commons with a dozen resolutions for the cessation of the slave trade. The bill, which abolished the slave trade in the British West Indies, did not pass until March 25, 1807, but Wilberforce chalked the delay up to the "goodness and glory of God." He visited Tsar Alexander and other potentates in Europe, urging abolition.

The slaves themselves resound as a great chorus of saints, singing their spirituals, so joyful, so hopeful, proving that even the harshest plantation could be transformed into a veritable beachhead of heaven itself. When they sang "Soon-ah will be don'-a wid de troubles ob de worl'" or "But some ob dese days my time will come," they latched onto a future hope, a righting of all injustices; at the same time they were buoyed by and sensed the presence of God now, no more so than when their voices were lifted in praise. When Sojourner Truth sang "There Is a Holy City," that heavenly Jerusalem seemed somehow truer, more real, than the embattled towns of America.

Hymns have a knack to sustain the faithful when the advent of God's kingdom seems to be delayed. A century after Yankees and Confederates bloodied the landscape over slavery, the project of securing rights for black Americans was far from complete. In April 1960, civil rights marchers were waiting for the mayor of Nashville to come out of the courthouse and meet with them, when a protester named Guy Carawan pulled out his guitar and began singing (with a classic Southern twang), "I'll Overcome Someday," an old song from the Baptist church tradition. Since the tune and words were so simple, the crowd picked it up quickly; and its destiny as the anthem of their movement ("We Shall Overcome") was assured, so beautifully did it express their resolve and faith.

SOMETHING BETTER TO SING

Some wonderful muse, probably God, plays these melodies in the souls of saints, and the rest of us are never the same. Newton's "Amazing Grace" was first of all autobiographical—but it also tells my story and yours too. Just the tune, just the first five notes resonate with something truly gracious that has been registered in our souls. It conjures up memories of my grandmother humming—and of the day of her funeral. In worship, I see a man thinking carefully about the challenge of the sermon, but it is the hymn, the verbalization of that transformation from being lost to the delight of being found that grabs and pulls him over the edge into discipleship.

God has blessed us with so many great hymns and hymn

writers. After worship one Sunday, eighteen-year-old Isaac Watts was complaining to his father about the deplorable singing and dreadful hymnody. His father said, "Well then, young man, why don't you give us something better to sing?" And he did, writing one hymn per week, to the enthusiastic reception of the congregation. Imagine sitting in a pew, sight-reading the local boy's hymn of the week, such as "O God, Our Help in Ages Past," "Joy to the World," "Jesus Shall Reign," "Am I a Soldier of the Cross," and "When I Survey the Wondrous Cross."

Fanny Crosby, blind by the age of six weeks, wrote over eight thousand hymns, including "Blessed Assurance," "To God Be the Glory," "Jesus, Keep Me Near the Cross," "Pass Me Not, O Gentle Savior," and "Rescue the Perishing," the last of which emerged out of her work at a New York city mission.

Horatio Spafford suffered the loss of his four daughters at sea when the SS Ville du Havre sank in 1873. Sailing to meet his wife, who survived the disaster, he wrote "It Is Well with My Soul," with its pain-riddled yet miraculously hopeful and faithful words. Philip Bliss, the great gospel music writer who traveled as an evangelistic crusader with Dwight L. Moody, set the words to music.

Cleland McAfee, pastor of First Presbyterian Church in Chicago in 1903, learned that two nieces had died of diphtheria. Somehow he sketched out the hymn, "Near to the Heart of God" and sang it outside his brother's quarantined house the day of the funeral.

"Silent Night," written by Joseph Mohr and set to music by Franz Gruber, was first performed on Christmas Eve 1818, in Oberndorf, Austria. Its power was nowhere better dramatized than during two World Wars when soldiers lay down their arms, crossed "no man's land," and joined their voices and hopes around the "holy infant so tender and mild."

Harry Emerson Fosdick, one of the twentieth century's stalwarts of the pulpit, wrote "God of Grace and God of Glory" at his summer home in Maine, planning its debut as the processional hymn at the very first worship service in the resplendent Riverside Church in New York on October 5, 1930. The church had been built near Harlem and was intended as a bulwark for a socially conscious Christianity that could criticize wealth and care for the poor.

In 1985 Natalie Sleeth wrote the exquisite "Hymn of Promise," which was immediately well received as a new hymn. Shortly after its composition, her husband Ronald was diagnosed with cancer. He asked her to have "Hymn of Promise" sung at his funeral. It moves many of us as well to sentiments of hope both today and as we contemplate our earthly end.

MILLIONS OF SOUNDS ASCENDING

On his deathbed in 1791, with a handful of friends gathered to wait and watch, John Wesley surprised everyone when he broke a long silence with, not words, but a song (from the hymn "I'll Praise My Maker While I've Breath" by Isaac Watts):

> I'll praise my Maker while I've breath;
> and when my voice is lost in death,
> praise shall employ my nobler powers.
> My days of praise shall ne'er be past.

Had we been able to ask Wesley what he might be doing two or three hundred years after his death, he would confidently have answered with those same words. To contemplate this unending employment in praise, the gradual addition of fresh voices, the grandest talents, the holiest hearts staggers the mind—and thrills the heart. In his play *Amadeus*, Peter Shaffer imagined Mozart thinking out his plan of composition:

> I tell you I want to write a finale lasting half an hour! A quartet becoming a quintet becoming a sextet. On and on, wider and wider—all sounds multiplying and rising together—and then together making a sound entirely new! ...I bet you that's how God hears the world. Millions of sounds ascending at once and mixing in His ear to become an unending music, unimaginable to us! That's our job! That's our *job*, we composers: to combine the inner minds of him and him and him, and her and her—the thoughts of chambermaids and Court Composers—and turn the audience into God.[14]

A VOICE OF GOD

If we consider the noblest musicians of history—Bach, Handel, Mendelssohn—their dedication to the sacred was their passion, but also their livelihood. Mendelssohn in fact, born Jewish, grandson of Moses Mendelssohn, was baptized Lutheran by his father in order to further his musical career. God works in dissonant, surprising ways—co-opting the artistry of music for divine purposes. In Shaffer's play Salieri overhears the *Adagio in E flat*—played from the first and only draft, completed entirely in Mozart's head. Staggered, Salieri speaks, "It seemed to me that I had heard a voice of God,"[15] or rather, that Mozart heard his rapturous music as if from heaven and merely wrote it down, as if by dictation.

Offended by Mozart's behavior yet awestruck by his talent, Salieri later said, "God needed Mozart to let Himself into the world."[16] Or as Karl Barth wryly suggested, "It may be that when the angels go about their task of praising God, they play only Bach. I am sure, however, that when they are together *en famille*, they play Mozart and that then too our dear Lord listens with special pleasure."[17]

Music lifts the heart and pierces the veil of the prosaic, ushering us into the ineffable yet certain presence of God, the mind-set and even the heart of God. Singers and poets assume their role in the great cloud of witnesses, providing the lyrics and the tunes to lead all of us in a chorus of praise. Dante's stated purpose was to "remove those living in this life from the state of misery and lead them to the state of felicity."[18]

HOW THE CHRISTIAN OVERCOMES EVIL

Or even, to protect us from danger. While still in seminary, Martin Luther King preached a sermon entitled "How a Christian Overcomes Evil," and it was punctuated by an illustration from mythology. The sirens sang seductive songs that lured sailors into shipwreck. Two men navigated those treacherous waters successfully—and King contrasted their techniques. Ulysses stuffed wax into the ears of his rowers and strapped himself to the mast of the ship and by dint of will managed to steer clear of the shoals. But Orpheus, as his ship drew near, simply pulled out his lyre and played a song more beautiful than that of the sirens, so his sailors listened to him instead of to them. Everything is at stake in the song we hear: safety or shipwreck, good or evil, enslavement or freedom.

And so, we turn now to another singer, a man who preached Martin Luther King's funeral, who lifted his voice with the saints of old on an unexpected stage: a prison cell.

CHAPTER SEVEN

PRIS⊙∏ERS

I can work for Him in prison as well as out.[1]

—CHARLES COLSON

One night in a Jackson, Mississippi, jail, back in 1961, a young civil rights protester with a stunning voice began to sing. The cells grew quiet, so enthralled were the prisoners by James Bevel's solo. The white prison guard demanded quiet, but Bevel sang on. The guard arrived at the door and asked for the radio: "No radios allowed in here—you niggers ought to know that." Bevel replied, "You ain't getting the radio—not this one." And then he continued singing "The Lord Is My Shepherd." The guard, uncertain if he felt anger or faith, walked away.[2]

This scene from Jackson reminds us of another prison and a more famous prisoner. Paul and Silas made their first intrusion onto the continent of Europe, landing at Neapolis and taking the Via Egnatia to Philippi where they were thrown into jail. The reason? "These men are disturbing our city" (Acts 16:20). The disturbance was primarily economic. A slave girl was making her handlers rich because of her uncanny ability to plunge into a trance-like state and voice cryptic words from the god Apollo. So when Paul healed the girl, they lost all hope of gain and had the apostle and his aide incarcerated, beaten by the lictors with rods, and shackled in stocks. In the pitch-black dark at midnight, far from weeping and trembling in anxiety, Paul and Silas were singing hymns. Tertullian has said that the legs feel nothing in the stocks when the spirit is in heaven.

BOETHIUS

Throughout the Middle Ages, Christians admired an author named Boethius for the wisdom he penned behind bars. Born around 480 into an aristocratic family with a pair of emperors and a pope among his kin, he emerged as one of the most powerful men, second in authority only to Theodoric, in the Roman empire. In 522, his two sons were elected consuls of Rome. No mere politician, he was a philosopher and scholar, translator of Aristotle, logician and teacher.

But Boethius was caught in the crossfire between warring theologians who turned to the Senate and emperor for support. He was imprisoned in Pavia and finally brutally murdered at age forty-four. While waiting to be executed he wrote *The Consolation of Philosophy*, a work of great artistry and genius, in which he rethinks his life, the nature of happiness, the fate of the soul. It is philosophy, the love of wisdom, that indeed is his consolation, no matter how he is treated. "The only way one…can exercise power over another is over [the] body and what is inferior to it,…possessions. You cannot impose anything on a free mind, and you cannot move from its state of inner tranquillity a mind at peace with itself and firmly founded on reason."[3]

In bondage, Boethius reflects on the atrocity of evil. "But the greatest cause of my sadness is really this—the fact that in spite of a good helmsman to guide the world, evil can still

exist and even pass unpunished."[4] Just before his death at
the hands of wicked men, he tenaciously holds on to a future
hope, a hope won through integrity and commitment:

> What do they care about reputation when the body
> grows lifeless in death which ends all things? If the
> whole of man dies, body and soul—a belief which our
> reason forbids us—fame is nothing at all, since the man
> who is said to have won it doesn't exist. But if the mind
> stays conscious when it is freed from the earthly prison
> and seeks out heaven in freedom, surely it will despise
> every earthly affair. In the
> experience of heaven it will rejoice in its delivery from
> earthly things.[5]

It is fascinating to consider how many of the great men
and women of history have done time in jail. The roll call
is impressive. Among the saints we have already considered, Dorothy Day, Francis of Assisi, and Martin Luther
King did prison stints, joining Gandhi, Galileo, Mandela,
and many others. Skim through Foxe's *Book of Martyrs*,
and recall that Bunyan wrote *Pilgrim's Progress* while in jail.
For religious folks, there is good biblical warrant for winding up in the slammer: Jacob's favorite son Joseph,
Jeremiah the prophet, and Daniel (whose cellmates were
lions!). The apostle Paul not only was incarcerated in cities
all over the Mediterranean, but he lived to brag about it.
Certainly his most eloquent letters were composed behind
bars. One of Rome's great churches, San Pietro in Vincoli,
boasts of a pair of treasures: Michelangelo's statue of Moses
and the chains affixed to Peter's wrists during imprison-
ment. The book of Revelation was written from the island
of Patmos, a penal colony. Jesus himself spent his last night
in a stone cell beneath the house of Caiaphas.

There are surprising lessons to be learned from

Christians in prison. How can your faith land you in jail? What happens to the soul of a prisoner? And what can the prisoner teach us about freedom?

MARTIN LUTHER KING JR.

On December 1, 1955, a black Methodist seamstress climbed on a city bus with a handful of others to go home after a long day at work. At a subsequent stop some white people got on. The driver, J.P. Blake, did what all drivers did, ordering the blacks in the fifth row to yield their seats and move to the back. "Y'all better make it light on yourselves and let me have those seats." Three moved, but Rosa Parks sat, edging snugly against the window. In part she was making history. But in part she just wanted to go home, and she was tired of giving in. Two policemen were summoned. She was fingerprinted and found herself behind bars. She prayed and waited. The authorities in Montgomery did not detain her for long. The spectacle of a humble, harmless woman of forty-two being forcibly restrained was an embarrassment. A month later she lost her job at the department store. In February she was arrested again for participating in a boycott. She was in Washington in 1963 and Selma in 1965 for the two greatest marches for civil rights.

She was an admirer of Martin Luther King Jr. who could have headlined our chapter on preachers. Like his father, he was a Baptist preacher. After coming to Dexter Avenue Baptist Church in Montgomery with no revolutionary aspirations at all, he was swept up in the aftermath of the arrest of Mrs. Parks—and it cost him jail time more than once. He was arrested for driving, for walking, for standing, for sitting. He chose on multiple occasions to stay in jail when he could have walked. Evil was confronted by a plan to fill up the jails with blacks who quite obviously were not violent but peaceable.

King had been fascinated with Mohandas Gandhi, who spent seven years in the raj's prisons for his peaceful pursuit of justice in India, and King proved to be his ablest imitator. Wendy Farley has said, "The profound moral integrity of Gandhi's or Martin Luther King's nonviolent struggles condemned their opponents by the contrast between them. These movements are especially powerful expressions of the work of compassion because they simultaneously empowered victims to resist their suffering and revealed to oppressors their guilt, struggling against the evil from both directions."[6]

The moral integrity of a prisoner. True freedom. King was free enough to stay in jail.

This Is Selma, Alabama

So problematical was the presence of King sitting behind bars in the Fulton County jail in Atlanta that governors, senators, the attorney general, and the President himself were swept up in trying to get him out. In Albany it was actually the police chief, Laurie Pritchett, who arranged for a black man to pay the fine to get King out of his jail. And the *New York Times* printed a letter from King on its front page, featuring big capital letters that exposed what was at stake: "THIS IS SELMA, ALABAMA. THERE ARE MORE NEGROES IN JAIL WITH ME THAN THERE ARE ON THE VOTING ROLLS."[7]

John Lewis, who later spearheaded a movement that registered over three million voters and became a congressman from Georgia, pointed to a photograph of himself as a young seminarian being released from prison in

Nashville. His face glowed with a dignity, a confidence: "I had never had that much dignity before. It was exhilarating—it was something I had earned, the sense of the independence that comes to a free person."[8]

In Birmingham King wrote, "What else is there to do when you are alone for days in the dull monotony of a narrow jail cell other than write long letters, think strange thoughts, and pray long prayers?"[9] He prayed, thought strange thoughts (such as, "I have wept over the laxity of the church; but be assured that my tears have been tears of love"), and wrote his famous and society-transforming "Letter from Birmingham Jail," a plea to the churches and the clergy to be who they are supposed to be, to show a little resolve and courage, to stand up for what is right.

Prisoners in our cloud of witnesses, from their stone floor pulpits behind iron bars, remind the church that our business is not inside the church but in the streets, where we are to seek out those points of conflict between our faith and a society out of sync with God. We are to risk everything, to confront evil, no matter what the cost. Perhaps the most powerful witnesses, sadly enough, are the unjustly persecuted.

WORLD WAR II

For Rosa Parks there was a happy ending, and she lived into old age, basking in the light of goodness and justice, a foremother of a cause that saw at least some success. Just over a decade before the bus boycott in Montgomery, many Christians were less fortunate and died in prison camps. Auschwitz claimed Edith Stein, a converted Jew, and Maximilian Kolbe, a Polish Franciscan who volunteered to die in place of a captured escapee (and husband and father) named Franciszek Gajowniczek. As we saw in chapter 5, Martin Niemöller landed in Sachsenhausen and Dachau for preaching on the theme, "God is my Führer!"

Halfway around the world, in what became the Pacific Theater, Toyohiko Kagawa was a lonely voice for Christ in Japan, a land that had greeted the message of Christianity three centuries earlier by crucifying missionaries. Born in 1888 in Kobe, Kagawa's parents died when he was only four. At age fifteen he enrolled in a Christian school with the stated intent of learning English. The textbook turned out to be the Bible, and a year later he was baptized—and immediately disinherited by the rest of his family. Into the slums of Kobe he went to preach, beginning a life of reaching out to the poor and destitute. When Japan flexed its military muscle in 1940, he denounced his nation's aggression and was jailed. After the war he led relief efforts for refugees and frequently was ranked with Gandhi and Schweitzer as heroes who combined prayerfulness, faith, compassion, and social action.

DIETRICH BONHOEFFER

Probably the most famous Christian prisoner of World War II was Dietrich Bonhoeffer. Born in 1906 into a comfortable, well-respected family, he studied for the Lutheran ministry with such panache that he was pushed to garner a doctorate. Just in his mid-twenties, his fame as one of the brightest theological minds in the world was soaring. But something happened. He chalked the shift up to his discovery (even after earning advanced degrees in theology!) of the Bible, finally taking it personally, finally "becoming a Christian"!

Bonhoeffer felt the dissonance between what he knew

about God and the church and the catastrophic direction being taken by his beloved Germany. Many Christians led the cheers for Hitler, reverencing the swastika as they would a crucifix. A few pastors stood up to Nazism; the Confessing Church was birthed in 1934. But Karl Barth was exiled from Bonn, and hundreds of pastors were jailed. Other clergy caved in, planning to lie low for the duration of the Nazi regime. Bonhoeffer by now was safely ensconced in London and then found himself traveling to New York.

But he was called by God back into the fray. Taking passage on the last ship to leave America for Hamburg, he returned to Germany. He secured an appointment to the Abwehr and under the veil of conducting legitimate business made contacts in Switzerland and Sweden to work for the overthrow of the Third Reich and for avenues to smuggle Jews out of Germany. The Nazis did not demand that he renounce his faith. Actually, the Gestapo's real target was Hans von Dohnanyi, Bonhoeffer's brother-in-law, whose secret papers later revealed Bonhoeffer's involvement in the ongoing plotting to assassinate Hitler. Bonhoeffer endured eighteen months in a military jail and another half year in a Gestapo cell. Just four days before the Allies liberated the Flossenbürg prison camp, Bonhoeffer was executed.

The Cost of Discipleship

During his years in jail, Bonhoeffer thought plenty about faith, about God, about life, and about the church. Even before prison, he had written *The Cost of Discipleship* in 1937 with its haunting first sentence ("Cheap grace is the deadly enemy of our Church"[10]); by 1943 he was bearing in his own body precisely that cost.

While in prison, at times he missed attending worship;

at other times he did not and wondered why. He observed the seasons and holy days as if on the outside. He saw more clearly than ever how "religion" is the mere garment thrown over the life of faith. He hopefully suggested a "religionless" Christianity, in the sense of a holistic style of life without a carefully segmented "spiritual" side bracketed off from one's life in the world.

Bonhoeffer went into prison with a profound grasp on things of the spirit. In his little book on the psalms, he spoke in such a beautiful yet challenging manner: "We confuse wishes…with prayer….Prayer does not mean simply to pour out one's heart. It means rather to find the way to God and to speak with [God], whether the heart is full or empty."[11] Or again, "If we are to pray aright, perhaps it is quite necessary that we pray contrary to our own heart. Not what we want to pray is important, but what God wants us to pray….The richness of the Word of God ought to determine our prayer, not the poverty of our heart."[12] As such, the psalms were a treasure to him; he saw that "they cast every difficulty and agony on God: 'We can no longer bear it, take it from us and bear it yourself, you alone can handle suffering.'"[13] He needed that treasure, and more, during two years under the Gestapo's thumb.

Genuine Freedom

Perhaps it is the saint's conduct in prison and the saint's thinking in seclusion that can reshape the lives of those of us on the outside. Joseph, unjustly imprisoned on a trumped-up charge from Potiphar's wife, was exemplary in his behavior in prison and out. Perhaps his wisdom, his ability to see things from God's perspective inside and outside, enabled him to bestow freedom on others, especially his fearful, despicable brothers (Gen. 45:1-8).

Bonhoeffer kept a prison diary (*Letters and Papers from Prison*) that has become a best-seller, and we may cherish his reflections. He learned a deeper sense of communion with the natural world, being enclosed behind bars — although he never mustered any warm sentiments for the flies in his cell. He learned to appreciate people, noting how "separation first makes it clear that often we take too little trouble to get together in normal times."[14] As never before, he grasped our common need for quiet and solitude: "You need to get right down to fundamentals, to come to terms with life, and for that you need plenty of time to yourself."[15]

Bonhoeffer can teach us about suffering, solitude, and freedom: "We have to learn that personal suffering is a more effective key, a more rewarding principle for exploring the world in thought and action than personal good fortune."[16] "We can have abundant life, even though many wishes remain unfulfilled."[17] "Nothing that we despise in the other man is entirely absent from ourselves.... We must learn to regard people less in the light of what they do or omit to do, and more in the light of what they suffer."[18]

As a corollary, Bonhoeffer learned to see God's involvement with us more clearly: "The Bible directs man to God's powerlessness and suffering; only the suffering God can help."[19] But this is no counsel of despair. "I believe that God can and will bring good out of evil, even out of the greatest evil."[20] He echoes those immortal words of Joseph, who managed with astonishing vision to see through the injustice of foolhardy brothers and an official's seductive wife to glimpse God's unthwartable plan (Gen. 50:20).

SINKING INTO THE MUD

We need to be careful to avoid the tendency to glamorize life in prison. At a safe distance and given the stalwart faith of men like Bonhoeffer, Boethius, and Bevel, we may imagine a room bathed in divine light, a happy place, a virtual antechamber of heaven itself. But it is only in modern times and only in a few countries that jails have had any decency about them at all. The cell where Jesus spent his last night was just a big hole cut down into subterranean rock, into which, onto which you were dropped in total darkness; rancid water puddled on the floor, and vermin kept you company. For most of our prisoners, beatings were more regular than food, which itself was some swill and a handful of moldy crusts. To suffer such a fate had to seem more abhorrent to all of them because of the nature of their guilt or innocence. To heed God's call, to obey God's word, to stand up with courage when others fled should have had some better recompense. It is in prison that the unfairness, the injustice of life is most keenly sensed. And it is from the prison cell that we hear witnesses bear ironic testimony to a profound faith by their complaints to God.

Hebrews 11 names the prickly prophet Jeremiah as one of its great exemplars of faith. Summoned at a tender age by God to a vocation he grew to dislike, Jeremiah infiltrated the corridors of power in Jerusalem to announce a hard word of judgment on King Jehoiakim. One stinging sermon denounced the king's lavish spending on his own palace while the people had nothing (Jer. 22:13-19). Another scathing tirade scoffed at the bogus, superficial religiosity of people who deluded themselves by believing that merely ambling about the Temple precincts insured God's blessing and protection (Jer. 7:2-15). When the powers that be tried to silence him, he dictated a thundering indictment, the reading aloud of which was interrupted when the king seized the scroll, shredded it with his own knife, and tossed it into the brazier (Jer. 36:4-32). When Nebuchadnezzar's military juggernaut ringed the city, Jeremiah—in a speech wholly lacking in patriotism—claimed the Babylonians were pawns in God's hands, the instruments of his judgment on an unrepentant city (Jer. 38:1-6). Jeremiah barely escaped with his life and was thrown into a cistern, where alone he struggled not to sink too deeply into the mud floor. His reward for telling the truth? A prison sentence.

At the same time, we are startled by the brightness of light that can emanate from the darkness of a cell. John of the Cross, who was born in 1542 and entered the Carmelite order in 1563, was imprisoned for his leadership of the Catholic reform movement in Spain. Before he died in disgrace, he wrote *The Spiritual Canticle*, an eloquent, soaring paean that lauds the grandeur and goodness of God. The fact that he escaped from jail with the rough draft in his hand tells us something about a faith that flowers in surprising places. He also wrote the *Dark Night of the Soul*, in which he beautifully explicated how God works in our souls not through what is obviously sweetness and light but in those hours that are darkness and despair: "If a man wishes to be sure of the road he travels on, he must close his eyes and walk in the dark"; and again, "The best fruit grows in land that is cold and dry." Perhaps it is from witnesses like Jeremiah and John, from the dank darkness of their prison cells, that we may learn how to stay with the darkness and pain in our own lives and discover a God who is not far removed from our isolation but is as close as the very loneliness that aches in our souls.

Archive Photos

NATAN SHARANSKY

A modern, even non-Christian, saint who has awakened an appreciation of freedom and commitment in many is Natan Sharansky, a Jew who was abducted by the Russian KGB in 1977. During nine years in prison in Lefortovo, then Vladimir, and then Chistopol, he suffered severe hunger, solitary confinement, brutal handling. His crime: advocating both free speech and an openness toward emigration.

When Sharansky finally was released, he still clutched in his hands a pocket book of Psalms. A pair of Soviet guards tried to confiscate his book, but he lay down in the snow and refused to move until they let him keep it. The Psalter had been a gift from his wife, Avital—but even more a gift from God. He had read and contemplated in depth those psalms. When he read, "Though I walk through the valley of the shadow of death, I will fear no evil: for thou art with me" (Ps. 23) or "Do not forsake me, do not abandon me, O God, my deliverer" (Ps. 27), his courage was bolstered, his identity confirmed, his hope assured. Because of this book, he saw the Gulag as "the place where I had emerged victorious, defended my freedom, retained my spiritual independence against the kingdom of lies."[21]

Freedom, independence. In some curious way, freedom and independence were attainable for Sharansky inside the Gulag in a way that eludes those of us on the outside. Shrewdly he observed:

> In freedom, I am lost in a myriad of choices....[A]n endless series of decisions...must be made: What to drink in the morning, coffee or tea? What newspaper to read? What to do in the evening? Where to go for the Sabbath? Which friends to visit?
>
> In the punishment cell, life was much simpler. Every day brought only one choice: good or evil ....Moreover, I had all the time I needed to think about these choices, to concentrate on the most fundamental problems of existence, to test myself in fear, in hope, in belief, in love. And now, lost in thousands of mundane choices, I suddenly realize that there's no time to reflect on the bigger questions. How to enjoy the vivid colors of freedom without losing the existential depth I felt in prison? How to absorb the many sounds of freedom without allowing them to jam the stirring call of the shofar that I heard so clearly in the punishment cell? And, most important, how...to retain that unique feeling of the interconnection of human souls which I discovered in the Gulag?[22]

THE FREEDOM TO BE FREE

Perhaps our glimpse behind the prison walls into the hearts of saints can remind us how desperately we need solitude. Freedom hinges not on cramming our time full of things we can choose to do and not on maximizing our options, but rather on time, on quiet, the space to concentrate on life, to plumb the depths of our souls, to explore the bigger questions, to sense our connection to others, to choose good and not evil. Nelson Mandela said after the legal dismantling of apartheid that "we are not yet free; we have merely achieved the freedom to be free."[23]

And the freedom to set others free. When Allan Boesak was in a Pretoria jail in 1985, imprisoned for battling against apartheid in South Africa, he thought back to the time he saw black teenagers dancing around a police car just after one of his church members had been arrested. They were singing:

> *Akanamandla, akanamandla, akanamandla uSatani!*
> *Sim'swabisile, Alleluia!*
> *Sim'swabisile, uSatani!*
> *Akanamandla, uSatani!*

"It is broken, the power of Satan is broken! We have disappointed Satan, his power is broken. Alleluia!" The police were confused and at the sound of the freedom song released their prisoner.[24]

THOMAS MORE

Freedom is exercised in commitment, not in doing whatever you want or going wherever you wish to go, but in letting yourself be wherever God places you, unwavering in your determination to be of one mind with God. Prison has taught this to some saints, among them Thomas More. Humanist, scholar, and statesman, More rose swiftly and became the second most powerful man in the realm of King Henry VIII. Erasmus wrote that More's soul was "more pure than any snow," although today we may shudder to note that More believed heretics and atheists should be executed. Zeal for purity has often led to violence. More resigned as chancellor in 1532, refusing to approve of the Act of Succession (which declared Henry VIII's marriage to Catherine of Aragon invalid, enabling the king to marry Anne Boleyn). More was not vocal, but his silence thundered throughout Europe. Charged with treason, he found himself in the Tower of London. He told Thomas Cromwell, "I do nobody harm, I say none harm, I think none harm, but wish everybody good. If this be not enough to keep a man alive, in good faith, I long not to live."[25] To his beloved but puzzled daughter Meg he declared his profound faith in God, that "a man may lose his head and have no harm."[26] With charcoal he wrote this verse on the stone wall of the Tower:

> Trust I shall God, to enter, in a while,
> His haven of heaven, sure and uniform.[27]

After blindfolding himself and uttering his last words, protesting that he was "the King's good servant, but God's first," More was beheaded.

He had undergone a major change while in the Tower of London. His political maneuvering and polemical ire vanished, and he instead wrote lovely devotional works that evidenced a profound personal intimacy with Christ. More's piety in prison was brought into the modern public eye by Robert Bolt, whose great play *A Man for All Seasons* is frequently produced and even wound up on film.

Two profound sentences placed on More's lips by Bolt capture the sense of what More was about, and both probe our own souls. When his daughter visits him, reminding him that freedom could easily be his, he remonstrates her: "When a man takes an oath, Meg, he's holding his own self in his own hands. Like water. And if he opens his fingers then—he needn't hope to find himself again."[28] Commitment. God uses our saintly prisoners to teach us about commitment. And we are called to an extraordinary commitment, not just because it is somehow noble, but because the Jesus we claim to be following embodied God's costly commitment to us. Of Norfolk and Cromwell More asks, "Dare we for shame enter the Kingdom with ease, when Our Lord Himself entered with so much pain?"[29]

CHARLES COLSON

We cannot say much about prisoners without remembering that our Lord urged his followers to visit them (Matt. 25:36). Not only may we learn profound truths about freedom and solitude from books about saints in prison, but we may actually go there to meet and talk with real people surprisingly very much like ourselves. Building a relationship behind bars will certainly change everyone involved.

One of this century's most effective prisoners has been Charles Colson. Notorious as Richard Nixon's "hatchet man" who would "run over his own grandmother" to re-elect the President, he tumbled swiftly from the corridors of power into a jail cell, caught in the undertow of Watergate.

In 1974, while Americans sat transfixed by the testimony of John Dean and the other conspirators before Sam Ervin's interrogation, Colson, already in trouble because of the Daniel Ellsberg case, was meeting with Tom Phillips, the president of Raytheon, who had recently been "born again." Phillips persistently yet lovingly urged Colson to accept Christ. After reading C. S. Lewis (*Mere Christianity*) and hearing Billy Graham preach in Madison Square Garden, Colson in great agony gave his life to Christ.

When his conversion hit the newswires, Colson was

lampooned mercilessly. On CBS, Eric Sevareid's commentary was strangely profound:

> Mr. Charles Colson, once the toughest of the White House tough guys, and a man believed by many to be standin' in the need of prayer as well as a good defense lawyer, Mr. Colson has made page one with the news of his conversion to religion. He is not repenting of any alleged sin of a juridical nature, but he does confess that he was just too big for his britches....A good many people here, anxious to believe in something, are quite willing to take Colson's change of heart as real.[30]

Colson, branded as inmate number 23226 at the Maxwell Air Base prison camp, became a model prisoner, deciding that "I have committed my life to Jesus Christ and I can work for Him in prison as well as out."[31] And so he did. He began praying and reading the Bible with his fellow inmates, observing how there truly are shades of good and evil in all people and believing that absolutely no person is ever written off, that by the grace of God there can always be a fresh start. Once he was released after eighteen months of incarceration, he demonstrated that his freedom had been continuous, before and after the bars were opened. His commitment to "work for Him in prison as well as out" has spawned probably the single most effective ministry to people in prison.

Finally we turn to the fact that some who are imprisoned are never set free but are executed, becoming to the eyes of faith not just statistics but martyrs. Over the centuries untold thousands of Christians have, under official sanction, been put to death. Their offense? Faith in Christ. Or, perhaps better: a willingness to be used by God. Maybe best of all: saints.

CHAPTER EIGHT

MARTYRS

*The saint is a medicine because he is an antidote.
Indeed that is why the saint is often a martyr; he
is mistaken for a poison because he is the antidote.*[1]

—G. K. CHESTERTON

The year was 112. Anxious to quell any potential unrest, the Roman emperor Trajan dispatched Pliny to Bithynia, not far inland from the Black Sea. A veteran politician whose uncle was asphyxiated by the eruption of Mount Vesuvius thirty-three years earlier, Pliny stumbled upon a secretive religious sect enjoying rapid growth but odd enough to threaten his sense of security. He gathered the so-called "Christians" together and urged them to renounce their faith. The alternative? Execution. Some protested they had never been part of this cult. Others chose to become "ex"-Christians. But some, painfully aware of the consequences, professed their faith, preferring death to denial. Today we call those who have been killed for their faith "martyrs."

REAL CHRISTIANS

Pliny's letter to Trajan is fascinating, especially these words:

> Those who denied being Christians now or in the past,
> I thought necessary to release, since they invoked our

156

gods according to the formula I gave them and since
they offered sacrifices of wine and incense before your
image which I had brought in for this purpose along
with the statues of our gods. I also had them curse
Christ. It is said that real Christians cannot be forced to
do any of these things.[2]

Real Christians! *Martyr* comes from a Greek word that
means "witness." Imagine a court of law. The jury, eager
to get at the truth, listens to testimony, weighing what witnesses have to say, measuring the authority of their words.
What better witness than someone willing to give everything, so noble is his or her cause?

The roll call of early martyrs is impressive. Stephen,
whose face shone like an angel, was the first to lose his life
because of Christ, stoned by a surging mob that included
Saul, who later became Paul (Acts 6:8-8:1). Herod Agrippa
had James, the brother of John, killed by the sword (Acts
12:2). Peter and Paul probably were executed in Rome
around the year 64; Peter is believed to be buried on the
Vatican hill, Paul on the Via Ostiensis just outside the walls.

None of this was entirely new. When Jesus was born,
Herod the Great's paranoia was such that he ordered all
infants and toddlers anywhere near Bethlehem to be killed
(Matt. 2:16). Warned of Herod Antipas's designs on his
life, Jesus still walked straight into Jerusalem (Luke
13:31). At the crest of the Mount of Olives with its pan-
oramic view of the city, Jesus lamented over Jerusalem
as the city that stoned the prophets (Matt. 23:37)—and
he had many such prophets in mind. A little-known
prophet Zechariah was killed by King Joash (2 Chron.
24:21). Isaiah, according to tradition, fled for the hills outside Jerusalem but was tracked down by the henchmen
of wicked King Manasseh and sawed in two (Heb. 11:37).

During the days of Jeremiah, the prophet Uriah was executed by king Jehoiakim (Jer. 26:23). Jeremiah himself was believed to have been stoned to death in Egypt, so pointed was his continuing protest against idolatry. Jesus' own friend and kinsman, John the Baptist, was beheaded by Herod (Matt. 14:1-12); he lost his head, as did Thomas More fifteen hundred years later, over a wedding.

AWAY WITH THE ATHEISTS!

More Christians fell during the reigns of Nero and Domitian, tied up in skins of wild animals and fed to dogs or burned as human torches. Polycarp, the venerable bishop of Smyrna, was burned at the stake in the year 156. Taunted by officials who urged him to cry, "Away with the Atheists!" (meaning the Christians), he wryly looked heavenward and said, "Away with the Atheists!" (meaning the Romans). The Proconsul persisted, "Curse Christ, and I will let you go." Polycarp's famous reply was this: "Eighty-six years have I served Him, and He has done me no wrong: how then can I blaspheme my King who saved me?...You threaten the fire that burns for an hour, and after a little while is quenched; for you are ignorant of the fire of the judgement to come....But why delay? Do what you wish."[3] Onlookers, including the Proconsul, were awed by the joy and peace on his face, even as he perished in the flames.

The great theologian Justin was beheaded; Ignatius was devoured by beasts, making two profound remarks: "I am beginning to be a disciple," and "I am God's wheat." He embodied Paul's image of death as a grain of wheat falling into the ground that eventually bears great fruit. And it was not just that Ignatius believed that he would personally gain eternal life by giving up his earthly life. He

foresaw the effects martyrs would have on the burgeon-
ing Christian movement and the world it sought to convert. As Tertullian wrote at the end of the second century,
"The blood of the martyrs is the seed of the Church."[4]

A PUBLIC SPECTACLE

The fact that martyrdom was usually a public show was
crucial. The Romans thought of gladiator fights as part
dissuasion, part entertainment. But making a spectacle of
a Christian leader, intended as a deterrent, merely exposed
the barbarity of Roman culture and gave voice to a faith
that did not shrink, even from a gruesome death. With a
maddening stubbornness, Christians fought like gladia-
tors in the arena for the faith, validating the key verse in
the book of Revelation: "For they did not cling to life even
in the face of death" (12:11). By contrast they were peaceful, attacking no one. Sham trials proved the guilt not of
the Christian to be martyred but of those who would cru-
elly inflict undeserved punishment on innocent victims.

God can use evil in this way. When four little girls
(Cynthia Wesley, Denise McNair, Carole Robertson, and
Addie Mae Collins) were killed in the bombing of the 16th
Street Baptist Church in Birmingham in September 1963,
their innocence shone brightly, as did the cruelty of
Southern racists. While these girls did not voluntarily give
up their lives for their faith, the date of their brutal murder is uncomfortably recent. The word *martyr* feels old,
like an antique in human history. Martyrdom is old, but it
has hardly vanished. Lest we construe martyrdom as somehow merely an ancient phenomenon, we must notice that
in modern times in places around the globe Christians are
still put to death for their faith.

Archive Photos

Dietrich Bonhoeffer

NO STORM TROOPERS IN HEAVEN

World War II revealed to humanity the sordid depths to which it is capable of sinking—and many great Christians lost their lives for their faith. We have already looked at the life and execution of Dietrich Bonhoeffer. His last words before he was hanged on April 9, 1945, were, "This is the end, for me the beginning of life." The camp physician wrote, "In the almost fifty years that I worked as a doctor, I have hardly ever seen a man die so entirely submissive to the will of God."[5]

Paul Schneider was a pastor in the Rhineland. Not long after Hitler's seizure of the dictatorship, a teenager, one of the "Hitler youth," died in a tragic accident. As Schneider was winding up his funeral sermon, the leader of the Nazi youth group strutted to the grave and proclaimed that the young man was now one of "Horst Wessel's heavenly storm troopers." Schneider firmly denounced this interruption, "This is a church service. There are no storm troopers in heaven!" Facing expulsion and threats on his life, he continued for three years to speak out and hold services in Christ's name. The Gestapo arrested him and deposited him in Buchenwald, a concentration camp where prisoners were forced to salute the swastika and pledge allegiance to Hitler each morning. Schneider resolutely refused, citing the salute as "idolatry." Tortured and cast into solitary confinement, he preached as loudly as he could from his cell—brief sermons to be sure, for the SS officers would beat him senseless. Finally on July 14, 1939, a strophantin injection put an abrupt halt to his preaching—and to his life.

Bishop OSCAR ROMERO *(El Salvador)* —

A Jesuit friend made this wise evaluation of Oscar Romero: "This man, timid, cowardly, became a prophet. He is the miracle God gave us."[6] In 1977 he actually was the government's "safe" choice for archbishop of El Salvador. Trained as a carpenter, he was conservative, feeling for a little while that his responsibility was to preserve the church as an institution at all costs.

But the brutal murder of his friend Rutilio Grande just three weeks after his installation shook him from his slumber. On the evening of his colleague's death, Romero spent the long, grievous night with Grande's parishioners and claimed that he was "converted" that very night. He became an outspoken advocate for the people, condemning governmental oppression in no uncertain terms. He was awarded a Swiss prize for peace and signed his prize money over to a hospital for indigent cancer patients just two days before his death. He knew his assassination was imminent. In the last two weeks of his life, he spoke these words to a Mexican reporter over the telephone, "My life has been threatened many times. I have to confess that as a Christian I do not believe in death without resurrection. If they kill me, I will rise again in the Salvadoran people." More personally he said, "God assisted the martyrs and, if it is necessary, I will feel him very close when I offer him my last breath. More important than the moment of death is giving him all of life and living for him." Or again: "If God accepts the sacrifice of my life, let my blood be a seed of freedom and the sign that hope will soon be reality."[7]

While saying Mass, just as he was lifting up the body and blood of the Christ he loved and served, Romero was shot in the chest, murdered by government operatives. The scripture reading had been John 12:24: "Unless a grain of wheat falls into the earth and dies, it remains just a single grain; but if it dies, it bears much fruit."

JEAN DONOVAN

Lest we misconstrue martyrdom as somehow merely a foreign phenomenon, consider the story of Jean Donovan.[8] Reared in Westport, an affluent suburb in Connecticut, with a comfortable life of superb academics and horseback riding, she earned a graduate degree in economics from Case Western Reserve and landed a lucrative job with Arthur Anderson in Cleveland. But she took her church involvement too seriously, especially what she learned from Father Michael Crowley. This priest had worked in the slums of Peru, Puerto Rico, and Harlem. She caught that contagion of passion for the poor, quit her job, and in 1977 found herself a lay missionary with the Maryknoll Sisters in El Salvador. After a two-year stint and with violence boiling up ever hotter in Latin America, Jean had the chance to settle back in the United States.

Yet, despite pleas from her parents and from her boyfriend, Doug Cable, a handsome young physician, Jean went back; she just couldn't leave the Salvadoran families she had met alone in their suffering. Her solidar-

ity with peasants being massacred was far more important
than anything she could do back in Cleveland or California.
On December 2, 1980, a national guardsman Colindres
Alemán ordered Joaquin Palacíos, Francisco Contreras,
José Canjura, Salvador Franco, and Daniel Ramírez to
put on civilian clothes and to take plenty of ammunition
for their G-3 rifles. They drove toward the airport and
hijacked a white minivan carrying four women: Dorothy
Kazel, Ita Ford, Maura Clarke, and Jean. The men
assaulted them sexually and then gunned them down. The
soldiers later claimed the women were "subversives."
Subversives indeed: women of compassion, daring to
protest the grossest injustice with food, tenderness, faith,
and courage. Jean was just twenty-seven, and her commitment and costly calling make it impossible for us ever
to dismiss suffering in some other part of the globe, impossible for us ever to imagine that we are somehow immune
to God's call to care.

In the modern world, as well as in antiquity, believers
are illegally arrested, tortured, and killed—and then they
just "disappear" and are reckoned as somehow "missing."
We do not know or remember their names. When Romero
was buried, forty more Salvadorans were executed by the
same government gangsters; him we remember, but their
faces and names are unknown to us. In the aftermath of
the Sharpeville uprising in South Africa, Steve Biko was
brutally killed; him we remember, but the names of the
forty-six others who died with him in detention escape us.
Francis Xavier was famous for his missionary endeavors
beginning in 1549 in Japan; yet we remember little of the
thousands of his nameless converts who were tortured,
beheaded, and even crucified for their faith.

THOMAS BECKET

Conflict between church and state has made many martyrs. In the last chapter we considered the fate of Thomas More, beheaded by Henry VIII. In many ways, More reminds us of another martyr who was born in 1120. Thomas Becket grew up in a bourgeois family but rose to prominence, achieving the powerful position of royal chancellor to King Henry II, whose domains became more vast after his marriage to Eleanor of Aquitaine. In 1162 after Theobald, the archbishop of Canterbury died, Henry gave the highest post in the English church to his friend Becket, assuming even more friendly relations with the church and support for all his policies would ensue. One day Becket was a layperson; the next day he was ordained; one day later he was archbishop of Canterbury!

At the consecration service, the Bible was (as was the custom) opened at random—and to the chagrin of the crowd, the verse on which chance alighted was that of Christ cursing the barren fig tree. To everyone's surprise Becket took this passage as an omen, a task to be undertaken, and began to call the church to fruitfulness, which subsequently involved him in a titanic struggle to stem the engulfing tide of secular power; king and court threatened to swallow up the church whole. Becket did not merely wink at the responsibility for priests to disdain pomp and glory. As we noted in chapter 1, Becket wore modest clothing, lived frugally, and even washed the feet of the poor. He read the Bible. He prayed. He was serious about his own penitence—and felt the king should be as well.

Becket had his own problems; he could be overly theatrical, inflexible, and was thought to be immensely insecure. But mostly he was zealous to serve the church faithfully, no matter what the cost. After a period of exile in France, he returned to England, more vehemently opposing the king and courting disaster for himself. After the annoyed King Henry made a passing remark that he wished someone would dispose of this headache, four knights, William de Tracy, Reginald fitzUrse, Hugh de Morville, and Richard le Bret, all hoping to rise in favor with Henry, rode off to Canterbury and assassinated the archbishop at the high altar of the cathedral.

The date was December 29, 1170. Church officials were deeply grieved, but they also seized on this disaster and made of Becket a great martyr, winning concessions from the guilt-ridden king. Six days later a rag stained with Becket's blood was applied to the eyes of a poor blind woman named Britheva—and her sight was restored. A mute priest named William was cured by a drop of the archbishop's blood, and a long succession of miracles were begun. Canterbury became England's most popular shrine.

THE HEART OF MARTYRDOM

Over the centuries martyrs have been venerated as the superheroes of the faith, as the ultimate Christians who quite literally fulfilled Jesus' words: "For those who want to save their life will lose it, and those who lose their life for my sake, and for the sake of the gospel, will save it" (Mark 8:35).

The early church believed that martyrs went straight to heaven, even to a specially reserved haven within paradise. Christians left on earth were intrigued by these saints and eagerly sought intimate contact with their souls. Relics of the martyrs became the hottest property in all of Christendom. Ashes, bones, skin, scraps of clothing, teeth

were encased in the altars of churches. Blood was metic-
ulously collected and applied to the sick and dying. The
shroud of Turin is in some bizarre way the ultimate "relic"
of the ultimate martyr. Anniversaries of the deaths of martyrs were solemnly commemorated at their tombs. Miracles
like those at Canterbury multiplied.

But in every age a danger has lurked in the shadows
of our fascination with martyrs. As with other saints we
have considered, if they are held in too high esteem, if they
are thought angelic and superhuman, then we may safely
insulate ourselves from the claim they may lay upon us.
As Jürgen Moltmann rightly said, "To turn remembrance
of the martyrs into a special cult of the saints can mean
putting the martyrs at a safe religious distance."[9] We need
not look to the martyrs for locks of hair, tunics, and fingernails. Instead, a different sort of fragment of the person is what we are after.

SOMETHING WORTH DYING FOR

Martyrs teach us many things, and chief among them is
the immense worth of our faith and at the same time the
worthlessness of much that pretends to have value. As
Saint Augustine pointed out, it is not the penalty that makes
true martyrs but the cause. To be sure, willingness to die
for a cause doesn't make it right. But people in all generations are strangely hungry for a treasure so precious that
death itself is not too high a price to pay to possess it. At
his trial Socrates taught that the purpose of life is not to
avoid dying but rather to avoid unrighteousness. Leo
Tolstoy claimed that the secret of life is not in staying alive
but in finding something to live for. By the time Martin
Luther King marched on Selma in 1965, many had died

in the struggle for civil rights. King spoke of the higher value of the truth: "I can't promise you that it won't get you beaten. I can't promise you that it won't get your home bombed. I can't promise you won't get scarred up a bit — but we must stand up for what is right. If you haven't discovered something that is worth dying for, you haven't found anything worth living for."[10]

This is the often forgotten plot of the story in Daniel 3:1-30. As we saw in chapter 1, Shadrach, Meshach, and Abednego did not plunge into the fiery furnace with some absolute certainty they would be delivered. They willingly climbed in because their zeal to live for God was more precious than life itself, because they could not tolerate any other god usurping the place of the true God in their lives. Listen once again to their bold witness: "If our God whom we serve is able to deliver us from the furnace of blazing fire and out of your hand, O king, let him deliver us. But if not, be it known to you, O king, that we will not serve your gods and we will not worship the golden statue that you have set up" (Dan. 3:17-18).

God perhaps will save us. But even if God doesn't, we will not compromise; we will not sell our souls to what is not truly God. So valuable is their life with God that even death is preferable to risking the ultimate and eternal good. Even if we are not called upon to sacrifice our lives in some foreign arena, we must weigh the glory God has promised as a vastly richer reward. We are cajoled into bowing down every day before the altar of television, in the corridors of the shopping mall, in the intricacies of our minds, in the thousand little decisions we make hourly. And it is our noble privilege to join the ranks of the martyrs and resolutely declare, "We will not serve your gods and we will not worship the statue you have set up" — no matter the cost.

OUR LEADER IS NOT DEAD

The faith of the martyrs reminds us of the future orienta-
tion of the Christian life. The world around us is the place
where we serve and give everything for Christ, but this
world is not the only world, not the final world. There is
a future, God's future, and we bank our hope squarely on
that future. Christians do believe that the Messiah has
come. But the vision of the messianic era, when the wolf
lies down with the lamb, when there is no more war or
injustice, when every knee bows and every tongue con-
fesses Christ—that day is not yet come. We take courage
because of the certainty of that hope and because of the
extraordinary faith of martyrs and saints who have pio-
neered the way for us into that future. Consider Martin
Luther King's last speech, the night before he was assassinated in 1968.

> Like anybody, I would like to live a long life; longevity
> has its place. But I'm not concerned about that now. I
> just want to do God's will. And He's allowed me to go
> up to the mountain. And I've looked over. And I've seen
> the promised land. I may not get there with you, but I
> want you to know tonight that we as a people will get to
> the promised land. And I'm happy tonight. I'm not
> worried about anything. I'm not fearing any man. "Mine
> eyes have seen the glory of the coming of the Lord."[11]

King and Andrew Young went back to the Lorraine Motel
and enjoyed a pillow fight. The next day, King was dead,
having lived a mere thirty-nine years—his mission incom-
plete, truncated, cut short. There is always an incom-
pleteness about our service to God. We never have enough
time or the right solution or sufficient resources. We are
hampered by our dim vision, our limitations, our wound-
edness. Reinhold Niebuhr was right when he said,

"Nothing worth doing can be accomplished in a single lifetime; therefore we are saved by hope."[12]

At the end of the day the future does not rest in our
hands but in God's. At King's funeral, James Bevel told
the crowd,

> There's a false rumor around that our leader's dead. *Our*
> leader is not dead. Martin Luther King is not our
> leader. Our leader is the man who led Moses out of
> Egypt. Our leader is the man who went with Daniel
> into the lion's den. Our leader is the man who walked
> out of the grave on Easter morning. Our leader never
> sleeps nor slumbers. He cannot be put in jail. He has
> never lost a war yet. *Our* leader is still on the case. Our
> leader is not dead. One of his prophets died. We will
> not stop because of that. Our staff is not a funeral staff.
> We have friends who are undertakers.[13]

God

Incidentally, the affirmation that God is our leader and
that the future belongs to God decided the fate of the so-
called "lapsed" Christians. In the third and fourth centuries, many Christians succumbed to pressure and denied
or cloaked their faith; some bribed a sleazy official or two
but tried to reclaim their status in the church once the danger was past. Priests especially were suspect: If your clergyman was discovered to have been a coward at the time
of trial, could you depend on the efficacy of your own baptism? or of the Lord's Supper you had received at his guilty
hands? The church wisely showed mercy. Jesus died, after
all, not for a band of courageous stalwarts but for all people, and most certainly for fearful, lethargic mortals swift
as Peter to deny, ready as Judas to betray. If truth and the
life of the church depend entirely on the goodness and perfection of mere mortals, we are in dire straits indeed. We
act. We strive for godliness, to be saints. But our lives are

*Are ye able said the
Master*

checkered, and the fruitfulness of our lives hangs entirely upon God, our leader.

GOD DOES NOT KILL

Part of what makes a death into martyrdom is the injustice of the act. It is the innocence of the martyr, the nobility of the cause in which the martyr is caught in some crossfire, that underlines that evil is very real, very dangerous, very lethal. While the blood of martyrs may be the seed of the church, while our faith may be bolstered by theirs, while their sufferings may be used by God for good, we must say out loud that God is not the executioner. It is not God's "will" that they die. God may take what is evil and bring good out of it; but evil is still evil.

When Christ was crucified, God was not on the side of the Romans, cheering on the centurion's detail. God did not urge Nero to use Christians as torches in his garden. God did not light the pyre beneath Polycarp, nor did God bless the Salvadoran military gunners who slew Romero and Donovan. James Earl Ray was not God's pawn, and Henry VIII was not doing God's will when he had Thomas More beheaded. Killing is always evil, even when the killers are pretending to be holy.

To our humiliation, Christians have martyred other Christians who didn't believe the right things, who were born in the wrong region, who dared to right a listing ship. In the fifteenth century the Council of Constance condemned and burned the Czech reformer John Huss much as his predecessor John Wycliffe had been executed. Mary Tudor, nicknamed "Bloody," burned close to three hundred Protestants in four years; Thomas Cranmer, Hugh Latimer, and Jasper Ridley were thrown in the Tower of

London and executed. John Calvin's Geneva witnessed the deaths of the theologically incorrect. On St. Bartholomew's Day in 1572, ten thousand Protestants were massacred in France. There is plenty of innocent bloodshed, and none of it is God's will, as even Abraham Lincoln, himself not a churchgoer, well understood. On March 4, 1865, thunderclouds were looming over the Capitol with its new iron dome as Lincoln delivered his second inaugural address to a war-ravaged country. He spoke eloquently of both Yankees and Confederates: "Both read the same Bible, and pray to the same God; and each invokes [God's] aid against the other....The prayers of both could not be answered; that of neither has been answered fully. The Almighty has His own purposes."[14]

Among the spectators that day was John Wilkes Booth. On Good Friday, just six weeks later, Lincoln was shot and killed. The violent of the world too swiftly attach the name of God to their own purposes, and the suffering and death that follow in their train are unutterable.

THE CRUCIFIED GOD

Perhaps Lincoln's thought about the purposes of the Almighty may help us rethink our own suffering and death. When a plane crashes or cancer strikes, many devout people claim that it is "God's will." Some sadists suggest that AIDS is God's punishment on homosexuals. But you might as well think of heart disease as God's punishment on those who indulge in a high-cholesterol diet or sniffles and coughs as God's vengeance on those who go out of doors in the cold. God is not sadistic. Why would God in some cavalier way select this person or that person to suffer? When we as a society became brilliant enough to put tons of metal full of passengers into the air at high speeds, we knew that some planes would crash. Cancer occurs for reasons scientists hopefully are in the process of unraveling. God is not a capricious killer.

But God is not uninvolved or remote from evil and death. Far from it. On November 16, 1989, at the university in San Salvador, six Jesuits, the housekeeper, and her daughter were murdered. Jon Sobrino, a famous Latin American theologian, would probably have been killed as well, had he not been traveling at the time. The killers dragged one of the bodies into Sobrino's room and accidentally knocked a book off his shelf, which then became soaked in blood. The book was *The Crucified God*, Jürgen Moltmann's eloquent book that portrays the suffering of Christ on the cross as the ultimate revelation of God's love. The pages of that blood-drenched book told how God suffered the death of his own son so that we might never suffer alone. In Christ God gathers up all the violence and bloodshed of history and shares our forsakenness, thereby fixing God forever to our pain and suffering, while shattering the specter of evil and the finality of death through his resurrection on the third day. The crucifixion is not the antithesis of God but the very revelation of the heart of God. Human suffering is not God's will but is surely enveloped and forever cradled in the heart of God.

In *The Crucified God*, Moltmann reflected on another of the atrocities of the twentieth century, the Holocaust, and was awed by Elie Wiesel's suggestion that he had seen God hanging on the gallows at Auschwitz. Wiesel was not in resignation saying God was dead—but rather that God was very present, full of grief, sharing the agony of the people. Moltmann went on to talk about martyrs:

[handwritten marginalia: Auschwitz]

[handwritten note at bottom: If you want peace work for justice]

It is necessary to remember the martyrs, so as not to become abstract. Of them and of the dumb sacrifice it is true in a real, transferred sense, that God himself hung on the gallows, as E. Wiesel was able to say. If that is taken seriously, it must also be said that, like the cross of Christ, even Auschwitz is in God himself. Even Auschwitz is taken up into the grief of the Father, the surrender of the Son and the power of the Spirit. That never means that Auschwitz and other grisly places can be justified.[15]

Moltmann

THE FLYER MUST FLY

As the first apostles faced suffering and martyrdom, a stunning notion emerged, expressed in Colossians 1:24: "I am completing what is lacking in Christ's afflictions for the sake of his body, that is, the church." When the faithful suffer for Christ's sake, they become actual participants in his own passion and in some mysterious way complete, or continue, or fulfill in the ultimate sense the work of salvation he accomplished on the cross. Paul also said that we are "always carrying in the body the death of Jesus, so that the life of Jesus may also be made visible in our bodies" (2 Cor. 4:10).

Our culture despises all suffering, and regards pain as something to be avoided at any and all costs. We associate God with what is pleasant; if there is agony, God must be absent or is surely busy arranging to alleviate all discomforts. But if the saints teach us anything, it is that following Christ does not solve all our problems. Actually we encounter a whole new set of problems. If God is to be found on earth, it is not necessarily in the places of bliss and ease but more likely in regions of sorrow. There is a cost to discipleship, and we need not be surprised if the afflictions of Christ begin to manifest themselves in our lives. We carry in our body the death of Jesus.

✳ the crux of this book

not only

The martyrs may teach us our most important lesson in life, which is how to die. In scattered places around the globe, Christians do still face death because of their faith. But all of us are mortal and face a certain death at some unspecified time in some frequently unexpected way. We are fragile, and there are secret disasters hidden in our bodies that may undo us at any moment, not to mention the omnipresence of external perils. The stark fact of our mortality is too blinding to look at for long—and yet we long to live in a way that we are prepared to die, that death would not catch us unawares with needed preparations undone.

Henri Nouwen had a brush with death in his late fifties. A delivery van slid on wet pavement and struck him. Massive internal bleeding left him in critical condition. This close call, along with the deaths of a handful of his friends and family members, nudged Nouwen to think more deeply than he ever had about death, his own, the deaths of those he loved. How can I befriend death? How can I live in whatever time I have left in a meaningful way? What can I leave that will be fruitful for others long after I am gone? His tragically shortened final years were fruitful, in part through the reflections he left for us in *Our Greatest Gift*, a brief but wise book in which he urges us to prepare for death not by staying busy with distractions but by attending to our relationships, especially our relationship with God, even daring to entrust ourselves into the hands of God as did the martyrs.

Nouwen

Henri Nouwen was fascinated by trapeze artists. He befriended a troupe of trapezists called the Flying Rodleighs. Once he asked the chief of the Flying Rodleighs how he managed to fly through the air and still catch on to the other guy on the swing. The answer?

The secret is that the flyer does nothing and the catcher
does everything. When I fly to Joe, I have simply to
stretch out my arms and hands and wait for him to
catch me and pull me safely over the apron behind the
catchbar....The worst thing the flyer can do is to try to
catch the catcher. I am not supposed to catch Joe. It's
Joe's task to catch me. If I grabbed Joe's wrists, I might
break them, or he might break mine, and that would be
the end for both of us. A flyer must fly, and a catcher
must catch, and the flyer must trust, with outstretched
arms, that his catcher will be there for him.[16]

trapezists

These images gave new depth to Nouwen's understanding of what Jesus meant in the hour of his death when he
said, "Father, into your hands I commend my spirit."

Death is a dark, fearful foe, to be sure. But because of
Christ, we can cope; we need not shiver in chilled terror —
for we have a catcher, and we need do nothing but fly. God
will catch us and draw us into the divine embrace, to be
with God forever. And in the same motion we will be
drawn into that great cloud of witnesses to enjoy eternal
fellowship with those we have loved, with those we miss,
with those to whom we needed to say something.

THANK GOD

When Socrates was condemned by the Athenians, he said
he looked forward to conversing with the great men of
the past. And so shall we. I want to hear the voice of John
Chrysostom. I want to look into the pure face of Thérèse
of Lisieux. I want to ask Martin Niemöller to describe the
exasperated look on Hitler's face. I want to squeeze the
hand of Dorothy Day and hear Clarence Jordan laugh.
I want to touch the wounds in Francis's hands and
watch Monica embrace her son. I want to sing bass in

the greatest choir ever, standing between Sojourner Truth
and Martin Luther as we mutually revel in the fact that
"we've no less days to sing God's praise than when we'd
first begun."

Mostly I want to say thank you. Thanks to Dietrich
Bonhoeffer for his courage. Thanks to C. S. Lewis for his
stories, thanks to Merton and Barth for their little and big
books. Thanks to Mother Teresa for picking up a hungry
child. Thanks to them all for changing my life, for reshap-
ing my soul, for whatever noble thoughts and instincts I
may have. I will look hard to find Floyd Busby, who never
knew he had the slightest impact on any of the little boys
who derided his teaching, and to tell him how his love for
Jesus has lived on in my life. I will find my grandfather,
Papa Howell, whom I caught praying and reading his
Bible, whose life and home were infused with stories of
faith, and I will climb again into his lap and thank him for
his life and love.

And I will not forget to thank God for dropping those
handkerchiefs. With the barbarian hordes threatening the
city of Hippo, Augustine put the finishing touch on *The
City of God*:

> And now, as I think, I have discharged my debt, with
> the completion, by God's help, of this huge work. It
> may be too much for some, too little for others. Of both
> these groups I ask forgiveness. But of those for whom it
> is enough I make this request: that they do not thank
> me, but join with me in rendering thanks to God.[17]

CONCLUSION

Like dwarfs standing on the shoulders of giants,
we see farther than they.

— BERNARD OF CHARTRES

Perhaps as this book draws to a close, you would chide me because of whom I left out. A misfit like Anthony, a servant like Vincent de Paul, or a master of the spiritual life like Benedict or Julian of Norwich. A teacher like Origen or Thomas Aquinas. A preacher like John Calvin or Jonathan Edwards. A prisoner like Watchman Nee or John Bunyan. A martyr like Lawrence or Joan of Arc.

We may think of other witnesses who have in their life and work thrown open windows into the heart of God. Rembrandt painted the return of the prodigal son, Caravaggio the call of Saint Matthew, da Vinci the Last Supper, Michelangelo the Creation, all in ways that are forever imprinted on our minds. Bach composed great arias, Handel the splendid *Messiah*, Mendelssohn the stupendous *Elijah*, Mahler the Resurrection symphony, Andrew Lloyd Webber the catchy *Jesus Christ Superstar*, all of which have drawn me into the chorus of the ages.

Scientists in their peculiar and perhaps unwitting way have expanded our horizons and thereby the scope of our sense of the marvel of God's creation: Copernicus shifted our cosmological perspective, so we could no longer think of earth, and certainly no longer think of ourselves, as the center of the universe. A foolish church tried to strike down Galileo and a substitute schoolteacher named John Scopes, but the truth about the universe does not threaten but only magnifies God. My faith has been deepened and refined by Annie Dillard, who has put in time watching hummingbirds and loons and glaciers, testifying that we live in a marvelous world, a profligate symphony of life, with the steady omnipresence of death, the ineluctable triumph of beauty and hope.

Flannery O'Connor once said that one of the delights of heaven will be that we will be able to converse with our favorite fictional characters. John Irving began his greatest novel by saying, "I believe in God because of Owen Meany"—and the quirky boy that dominates *A Prayer for Owen Meany* has compelled me to think about my life, vocation, and destiny more profoundly. The subterranean struggles of Pat Conroy's characters, the personality transformations of Adam Bede and Silas Marner unveiled by George Eliot, the ugly yet strangely hopeful souls of Hazel Motes and Mrs. Turpin so generously told by Flannery O'Connor—these people inhabit my soul and surprisingly nudge me toward God, toward a more thoughtful discipleship. Of course I think of my grandparents, a couple of seminary professors, a roommate, a couple of neighbors, the minister who looked at me one day and asked, "Have you ever thought about going into the ministry?" I turned my head to see whom he might be addressing.

A WILLINGNESS TO BE AWED

Perhaps you have a name, a face in your mind, someone who should be named in this book. But on the other hand, maybe you can't think of anybody. If so, you probably are not alone. We live in a culture of so much nonsense, in an atmosphere where unholiness, superficiality, and self-indulgence are glorified. We have grown cynical as a people. The few stalwarts in whom we have dared to hope have betrayed us. A president or two, a famous clergyman or two, brimming with idealism and talk of great things but exposed as charlatans or liars or adulterers. We perhaps wisely have suspicions about those who talk of grand adventures of sacrifice and service, because we have been taken advantage of too often. We are unwilling to be awed.

This book is an invitation, perhaps a mnemonic device, to restore in us that ability to be awed, to become the kind of people who select their role models carefully and then with great abandon pursue what Thomas à Kempis called the imitation of Christ. I want to be like Christ in the same way Francis was like Christ. I want to serve with the same zeal I see in Dorothy Day or Mother Teresa. I want to love Christ the way Thérèse did. I want to think faithfully about Christ the way Augustine and Luther did. I want to get on people's nerves the way Clarence Jordan did. I want my faith to cost me something precious, as it cost Dietrich Bonhoeffer, Thomas More, Jean Donovan, Oscar Romero. Murray Bodo put it like this:

> There is something about Francis himself and the *way* he lives the Gospel that has an irresistible attraction for me. He dares to live the Gospel the *way* I would like to live it, and he loves Jesus the way anyone would like to be loved.... But there is something more. Francis makes *me* feel loved; he makes me feel that I matter, that I am exciting and interesting and full of potential.[1]

How remarkable that someone who lived eight centuries ago could touch me so. And how true—that I do feel loved, that I matter, that I am brimming with possibilities. That

is why Francis and his friends through the ages lay claim
to me, why their witness decides the case against society's
glitter and in favor of God, why it is impossible to become
acquainted with them and not go out and change things
in my life and in the world.

THE GOOSE CHURCH

The nineteenth-century philosopher Søren Kierkegaard,
who could easily have headed our list of misfits, devised a
parable of how we ignore the claim of the saints. Imagine
a community of talking geese. Every Sunday the geese
came to worship, and the gander preached a stirring sermon about the lofty destiny of the goose, how God had
given the goose wings to fly away to foreign lands and fair
climates. The goose's true home was in the sky; it was only
a stranger on the earth. Throughout the sermon the geese
curtsied and voiced their approval. But when worship was
over, the geese waddled back home and grew more plump.
During the week they would recount what happened to
one poor goose who dared to make serious use of his
wings—and his terrible demise. Of course on Sundays this
went unmentioned, for it would then become clear that
their worship was mere foolishness. The gander would
preach once more of the lofty destiny, and the geese would
waddle home and grow more plump.[2]

   The stories we have considered in these pages are proof
that we have wings and that we need not waddle through
the balance of our lives. The saints are those who heard the
plea, "You shall love the Lord your God with all your heart,
soul, mind, and strength," and they discovered their wings
and took flight. They believed there was treasure in heaven
and so became poor. They sold everything for the pearl of

great price. They glimpsed the shape of the life to which we are all called and let it become flesh in them. Far from crying out about the high cost of discipleship, they knew that the higher cost was nondiscipleship; and they were unwilling to settle for less than that to which God was inviting them. Romano Guardini described it well:

> But they all have one thing in common: the demands which the love of God makes upon their hearts causes them to transcend the ordinary mass of human beings and to accomplish something altogether exceptional. This alone makes them witnesses of the eternally new greatness which Christ alone has made possible in history. They refract, so to speak, the light of divine simplicity into forms of infinite variety. They are the models, they show the aims and the paths of sanctity, they arouse the forces which will continue to work for centuries, their lives describe the outlines of which other Christians will simply fill in the details with imitation and accomplishment.[3]

The saints we have considered did not define in advance what they wanted God to do for them. Rather, they were willing to do whatever. Wherever God led them, that is where they wanted to go.

And so they clamor for our attention, challenging each of us to go, to love, to serve, even to die. Even if they have themselves died, they live on in their stories and also in the heart of God and are busy cheerleading for you and me, energetically shouldering our weariness, whispering a powerful word of hope. And so we try, perhaps for the first time, striking out in faith, into the darkness, eager to go where they have gone, hopeful to discover wings that have amazingly lain undetected all these years. The possibilities are virtually unlimited—because they are God's possibilities.

THE SECRET OF SAINTHOOD

What is the secret of sanctity, of sainthood, of nobility? Were it genetic we would clone a few more Francises. Parenting seems to be a factor. We could argue that the real saints in our story are Pica, the mother, who took sides with Francis against his father, or Monica whose prayers surely issued in Augustine, or Louis Martin who raised a bevy of daughters (including Thérèse) who wanted above all to be like their father in devotion to prayer and compassion, or Martin Luther King Sr. who set the bar high for his son. Yet saints emerge from dysfunctional families or families with no particular distinction religiously speaking: the Luthers, Days, Jordans, and Mertons, not to mention terrible fathers like Augustine's Patricius or Francis's Pietro.

Suffering may be a paradoxically positive factor. Most of our saints have suffered or at least have discovered that their suffering is the crucible in which they realize God's call, God's reliability, God's gifts. Francis and Teresa of Avila were fragile and sickly. Thérèse and Merton bore the deaths of parents and siblings at a tender age. Certainly in times of persecution, the faith of Christians has been tested, refined, deepened. When it is convenient to go to church, when there is no pressure on the faithful, the risks are immense that we will trivialize our faith into something innocuous.

Occurrences we might chalk up to chance are so pivotal in the lives of saints that we may discern the finger of God dipping into history. Zélie Martin was determined to live as a nun, but her application was turned down; otherwise we would have no Thérèse. Political turmoil in Germany coincided with the invention of the printing press, which in no small way made Luther's reformation so timely.

Sojourner Truth was randomly purchased on the slave trading block by an abolitionist family. While on vacation, Millard Fuller happened to stop off in Georgia to see friends who happened to know Clarence Jordan. Chance, perhaps. Or perhaps God was engineering a circumstance or two.

THE ONLY SOLUTION

Almost always for the saints there are those who mentor them toward greatness. Augustine had Bishop Ambrose of Milan as his preacher and exemplar. Luther had Johann von Staupitz as pastor and advisor. Fuller had Jordan. Indeed, the church is always there as midwife, bringing new children of God into the world. Admittedly the church has its foibles and is repeatedly unheroic when heroism is called for. Karl Barth and Martin Niemöller were mortified by the rallying of churches behind Hitler. Martin Luther King and Clarence Jordan were grieved by the church's shrill defense of segregation. Isaac Watts was bored in worship, and John Wesley and George Whitefield had to preach outside the churches in part because the preachers would not permit them inside their sanctuaries. Dorothy Day joined the church, not because she appreciated what she saw of it, but because she loved what it was supposed to be.

What greater witness to the power of God could there be than the way such an unheroic church manages to call forth great heroes! Indeed, as we say in the liturgy, "The Church is of God, and will be preserved to the end of time." Not one of the saints has been a solo act. In our era many believe you can be a Christian without the church, and perhaps you can be a better Christian without the hypocritical complications of church life. But the saints urge us to be in the church, engaged with other Christians in prayer, worship, and service. The church has a book, a set of prayers and practices, and its saints; it is our privilege to be shaped by its treasury. The church is a place where we can stand. The church supports us, ennobles, and encourages us.

Saints need saints, and we need the institution of the church, because we know whose church it is. In the church we recognize that Augustine was right when he said, "Really great things, when discussed by little [people], can usually make such [ones] grow big."[4] Without the church, there would be no saints—and we would not even hear God's witnesses, would never glimpse those lovely hand-kerchiefs God tosses out of love toward us. We need one another; we are all the time helping one another toward God. Dorothy Day concluded her 1952 autobiography by saying, "We have all known the long loneliness and we have learned that the only solution is love and that love comes with community."[5]

For it is in community with God, with the church, with all of God's children, that we belong. Mother Teresa once said, "I am Albanian by birth. Now I am a citizen of India. I am also a Catholic nun. In my work, I belong to the whole world. But in my heart, I belong to Christ."[6] My heart, my work—that is what matters. And so may we gather with the saints of yesteryear around the deathbed of the poor fragile misfit Saint Francis and hear him utter God's word to each of us: "I have done what is mine to do; may Christ teach you what is yours to do."

NOTES

INTRODUCTION

1. FrederickBuechner, *Wishful Thinking: A Seeker's ABC* (San Francisco: HarperSanFrancisco, 1993).

CHAPTER ONE: MISFITS

1. G. K. Chesterton, *Saint Thomas Aquinas* (Garden City, New York: Image Books, 1956), 24.
2. Flannery O'Connor, *A Good Man Is Hard to Find* (New York: Harcourt Brace Jovanovich, 1955), 26.
3. Chesterton, *Saint Thomas Aquinas*, 43.
4. There are many biographies of Saint Francis. The earliest stories of his life are conveniently put together in *The Little Flowers, Legends, and Lauds*, ed. Otto Karrer, trans. N. Wydenbruck (London: Sheed and Ward, 1947).
5. Karrer, *The Little Flowers*, 8.
6. Murray Bodo, *The Way of St. Francis: The Challenge of Franciscan Spirituality for Everyone* (New York: Image Books, 1984), 105–106.
7. Arnaldo Fortini, *Francis of Assisi*, trans. Helen Moak (New York: Crossroad, 1981), 557.
8. The stories and quotes in this section come from two good books about Jordan: Dallas Lee, *The Cotton Patch Evidence* (New York: Harper and Row, 1971); and Henlee H. Barnette, *Clarence Jordan: Turning Dreams into Deeds* (Macon, Ga.: Smith & Helwys, 1992).
9. Barnette, *Clarence Jordan*, 9.
10. Frye Gaillard, *If I Were a Carpenter* (Winston-Salem, N.C.: John F. Blair, 1996), 8–11.
11. Ibid., 13.
12. Cited in James Wm. McClendon Jr., *Biography as Theology* (Philadelphia: Trinity Press International, 1990), 110–111.
13. Ibid., 112.
14. McClendon., *Biography as Theology*, 103.
15. Barnette, *Clarence Jordan*, 33–34.
16. Lee, *Cotton Patch Evidence*, 11.
17. Luther's *Works*, 3:81 as cited in Douglas John Hall, *Thinking the Faith* (Minneapolis, Minn.: Augsburg Fortress, 1989), 108.
18. Bodo, *The Way of St. Francis*, 21.
19. Chesterton, *Saint Thomas Aquinas*, 23–24.
20. Bodo, *The Way of St. Francis*, 10.

21. Henri J. M. Nouwen, *¡Gracias!: A Latin America Journal* (San Francisco: Harper & Row, 1983), 11.

CHAPTER TWO: SERVANTS

1. Kathryn Spink, *Jean Vanier and l'Arche: A Communion of Love* (New York: Crossroad, 1991), 194.
2. Among the many biographies I might recommend Anne Sebba, *Mother Teresa: Beyond the Image* (New York: Doubleday, 1997).
3. Mother Teresa, *My Life for the Poor*, eds. José Luis González-Balado and Janet N. Playfoot (San Francisco: Harper & Row, 1985), 78–79.
4. Ibid., 15.
5. Ibid., 8.
6. Mother Teresa, *Words to Love By* (Notre Dame: Ave Maria Press, 1983), 80.
7. Chesterton, *Saint Francis of Assisi*, 47, 40.
8. Karrer, *The Little Flowers*, 36.
9. Ibid., 12.
10. Spink, *Jean Vanier and l'Arche*, 45.
11. Ibid., 67.
12. Ibid., 68.
13. Jim Forest, *Love Is the Measure: A Biography of Dorothy Day*, rev. ed. (Maryknoll, N.Y.: Orbis Books, 1994), 77.
14. For an excellent biography see Jim Forest, *Love Is the Measure* and also Day's autobiographical writings, especially *The Long Loneliness* (San Francisco: HarperSanFrancisco, 1980).
15. Forest, *Love Is the Measure*, 59
16. Robert Coles, *Dorothy Day: A Radical Devotion* (Reading, Mass.: Addison-Wesley, 1987), 28.
17. Forest, *Love Is the Measure*, 135.
18. Coles, *Dorothy Day*, 16.
19. The story of Millard Fuller and the phenomenal work of Habitat for Humanity is beautifully told in Frye Gaillard's book, *If I Were a Carpenter* (Winston-Salem, N.C.: John F. Blair, 1996).
20. Lee, *Cotton Patch Evidence*, 214.
21. *A Testament of Hope: The Essential Writings and Speeches of Martin Luther King, Jr.*, ed. James M. Washington (San Francisco: HarperSanFrancisco, 1991), 282.
22. Jimmy Carter, *Living Faith* (New York: Random House, 1996), 255.
23. Day, *The Long Loneliness*, 243.
24. Forest, *Love Is the Measure*, 67.
25. Ibid., 153–54.
26. Ibid., 154.

CHAPTER THREE: PRAYERS

1. Kenneth Leech, *True Prayer: An Invitation to Christian Spirituality* (Harrisburg, Penn.: Morehouse, 1995), 36.
2. Saint Augustine, *The Confessions of St. Augustine*, trans. John K. Ryan (Garden City, N.Y.: Image Books, 1960), 92.

3. *The Life of Teresa of Jesus*, trans. E. Allison Peers (Garden City, N.Y.: Image Books, 1960), 71.

4. Guy Gaucher, *The Story of a Life: St. Thérèse of Lisieux* (San Francisco: HarperSanFrancisco, 1987), 51.

5. Ibid., 148.

6. Ibid., 163.

7. Ibid., 146.

8. Ibid., 197

9. Thomas à Kempis, *The Imitation of Christ*, trans. Leo Sherley-Price (Middlesex: Penguin, 1952), 180–81.

10. Thomas Kelly, *A Testament of Devotion* (San Francisco: HarperSanFrancisco, 1992), 9.

11. Thomas Merton, *The Seven Storey Mountain* (New York: Harcourt Brace Jovanovich, 1976), 83.

12. Ibid., 404.

13. Thomas Merton, *Zen and the Birds of Appetite* (New York: New Directions, 1968), 76.

14. Thomas Merton, *Spiritual Direction and Meditation and What Is Contemplation?* (Wheathampstead-Hertfordshire: Anthony Clarke, 1975), 85.

15. Thomas Merton, *New Seeds of Contemplation* (New York: New Directions, 1962), 35.

16. Merton, *Spiritual Direction*, 90.

17. Thomas Merton, *Contemplative Prayer* (New York: Image Books, 1996), 37.

18. Merton, *New Seeds of Contemplation*, 97.

19. Ibid., 24.

20. Henri J. M. Nouwen, *The Road to Daybreak: A Spiritual Journey* (New York: Image Books, 1990), 2.

21. Ibid., 4.

22. Ibid., 22.

23. Ibid., 19.

24. Gaucher, *The Story of a Life*, 193.

25. Augustine, *The Confessions*, 224–25.

26. Nouwen, *Road to Daybreak*, 117.

27. Joseph Cardinal Bernardin, *The Gift of Peace: Personal Reflections* (Chicago: Loyola Press, 1997), 67.

28. Jean Leclercq, *The Love of Learning and the Desire for God*, trans. Catharine Misrahi (New York: Fordham University Press, 1982), 266.

CHAPTER FOUR: TEACHERS

1. Quoted by Dorothy Day in *The Long Loneliness*, 17.

2. Henri Crouzel, *Origen*, trans. A. S. Worrall (Edinburgh: T. & T. Clark, 1998), 28.

3. Karl Barth, *The Word of God and the Word of Man*, trans. Douglas Horton (New York: Harper & Row, 1957), 186.

4. Barth, *The Word of God*, 196.

5. Eberhard Busch, *Karl Barth: His Life from Letters and Autobiographical*

Texts, trans. John Bowden (Philadelphia: Fortress Press, 1976), 496.

6. Ibid., 489.
7. A helpful summary of Lewis's life and his work is Walter Hooper, *C. S. Lewis: A Companion and Guide* (San Francisco: HarperSanFrancisco, 1996).
8. Hooper, *C. S. Lewis*, 14.
9. C. S. Lewis, *The Screwtape Letters* (New York: Macmillan Publishing Co., 1961), 3.
10. Hooper, *C. S. Lewis*, 397.
11. On his life and thinking, see Peter Brown, *Augustine of Hippo: A Biography* (Berkeley: University of California, 1967).
12. Charles Williams, *The Descent of the Dove: A Short History of the Holy Spirit in the Church* (Vancouver: Regent College Publishing, 1997), 164.
13. A popular, readable biography is Roland H. Bainton, *Here I Stand: A Life of Martin Luther* (New York: Abingdon-Cokesbury Press, 1950).
14. Bainton, *Here I Stand*, 147.
15. Ibid., 21.
16. Ibid., 45.
17. Ibid., 54.
18. Ibid., 80.
19. Ibid., 183.
20. Ibid., 185.
21. David C. Steinmetz, *Luther and Staupitz* (Durham: Duke University, 1980), 57.
22. Bainton, *Here I Stand*, 82–83.
23. Gerhard Ebeling, *Luther: An Introduction to His Thought*, trans. R. A. Wilson (Philadelphia: Fortress, 1970), 66–67.
24. Williams, *Descent of the Dove*, 172.
25. David Halberstam, *The Children* (New York: Fawcett Books, 1998), 62.

CHAPTER FIVE: PREACHERS

1. Augustine, *Homilies on the Gospel of John* from *Nicene and Post-Nicene Fathers*, vol. 7, ed. Philip Schaff (Peabody: Hendrickson, reprint 1994), 254.
2. C. S. Lewis, *The Weight of Glory* (New York: Simon & Schuster, 1996), 26.
3. Ibid., 39.
4. Stuart C. Henry, *George Whitefield: Wayfaring Witness* (New York: Abingdon Press, 1957), 163.
5. Billy Graham, *Just As I Am* (New York: Harper paperbacks, 1997), 694.
6. Neil Postman, *Amusing Ourselves to Death: Public Discourse in the Age of Show Business* (New York: Penguin Books, 1985), 118.
7. Ibid., 116–17.
8. Sinclair Lewis, *Elmer Gantry* (New York: Signet, 1967), 9.
9. Ibid., 416.
10. Karrer, *The Little Flowers*, 27.

11. *A Testament of Hope* (San Francisco: HarperCollins, 1986), 282.
12. J. N. D. Kelly, *Golden Mouth: The Story of John Chrysostom—Ascetic, Preacher, Bishop* (Ithaca: Cornell University Press, 1995), 98.
13. Ibid., 99.
14. Quoted with a good discussion in Justo L. González, *Faith and Wealth: A History of Early Christian Ideas on the Origin, Significance, and Use of Money* (San Francisco: Harper & Row, 1990), 210.
15. Ibid., 203.
16. Ibid., 211.
17. Kelly, *Golden Mouth*, 60.
18. Nell Irvin Painter, *Sojourner Truth: A Life, A Symbol* (New York: W. W. Norton, 1996), 106..
19. Ibid., 167.
20. Ibid., 168.
21. Ibid., 126.
22. Ibid., 125.
23. Ibid., 160.
24. Ibid., 161.
25. Clarissa Stuart Davidson, *God's Man: The Story of Pastor Niemöller* (New York: Ives Washburn, 1959), p. 59.
26. Ibid., 239.
27. David Halberstam, *The Fifties* (New York: Willard Books, 1993), 544.

CHAPTER SIX: SINGERS
1. Robert Bly, *The Sibling Society* (Reading, Mass.: Addison-Wesley, 1996), 238.
2. Thomas Merton, *Praying the Psalms* (Collegeville, Minn.: The Liturgical Press, 1956), 7.
3. Martin Luther, *Word and Sacrament* I, LW35, ed. Theodore Bachmann (Philadelphia: Muhlenberg Press, 1960), 255.
4. *The Portable Dante*, trans. and ed. Mark Musa (New York: Penguin Books, 1995), 3.
5. Ibid., 14.
6. Ibid., 191.
7. Ibid., 410.
8. Ibid., 584.
9. *I, Francis*, trans. Robert R. Barr (Maryknoll, N.Y.: Orbis Books, 1985), 106.
10. Bainton, *Here I Stand*, 269.
11. Quoted in Richard Foster, *Streams of Living Water: Celebrating the Great Traditions of Christian Faith* (San Francisco: HarperSanFrancisco, 1998), 237.
12. Quoted in Stanley Ayling, *John Wesley* (Nashville: Abingdon Press, 1979), 305.
13. Kenneth W. Osbeck, *101 More Hymn Stories* (Grand Rapids: Kregel Publications, 1985), 13.
14. Peter Shaffer, *Amadeus* (New York: Harper & Row, n.d.), 64.

15. Ibid., 22.
16. Ibid., 56.
17. Karl Barth, *Wolfgang Amadeus Mozart*, trans. Clarence K. Pott (Grand Rapids, Mich.: William B. Eerdmans, 1986), 23.
18. *The Portable Dante*, xxx.

CHAPTER SEVEN: PRISONERS

1. Charles W. Colson, *Born Again* (Old Tappan, N.J.: Chosen Books, 1976), 250.
2. Halberstam, *The Children*, 342.
3. Boethius, *The Consolation of Philosophy*, trans. V. E. Watts (Middlesex: Penguin Books, 1969), 70.
4. Ibid., 116.
5. Ibid., 75.
6. Wendy Farley, *Tragic Vision and Divine Compassion: A Contemporary Theodicy* (Louisville: Westminster/John Knox Press, 1990), 121.
7. Halberstam, *The Children*, 498.
8. Ibid., 140.
9. *A Testament of Hope*, 302.
10. Dietrich Bonhoeffer, *The Cost of Discipleship*, trans. R. H. Fuller (New York: Macmillan, 1963), 45.
11. Bonhoeffer, *Psalms: The Prayer Book of the Bible*, trans. James H. Burtness (Minneapolis: Augsburg, 1970), 9–10.
12. Ibid., 14–15.
13. Ibid., 48.
14. Bonhoeffer, *Letters and Papers from Prison*, ed. Eberhard Bethge (New York: Macmillan, 1971), 77.
15. Ibid., 271.
16. Ibid., 17.
17. Ibid., 234.
18. Ibid., 10.
19. Ibid., 361.
20. Ibid., 11.
21. Natan Sharansky, *Fear No Evil*, trans. Stefani Hoffman (New York: Random House, 1988), 229.
22. Ibid., 423.
23. Nelson Mandela, *Long Walk to Freedom: The Autobiography of Nelson Mandela* (Boston: Back Bay Books, 1995), 624.
24. Allan Boesak, *Comfort and Protest: Reflections on the Apocalypse of John of Patmos* (Philadelphia: The Westminster Press, 1987), 60–62.
25. Anthony Kenny, *Thomas More* (Oxford: Oxford University, 1983), 81.
26. Ibid., 80.
27. Ibid., 82.
28. Robert Bolt, *A Man for All Seasons: A Play in Two Acts* (New York: Vintage Books, 1962), 81.
29. Ibid., 87.

30. Colson, *Born Again*, 171.
31. Ibid., 250.

CHAPTER EIGHT: MARTYRS

1. Chesterton, *Saint Thomas Aquinas*, 23.
2. Translated with a good discussion by M. Eugene Boring, *Revelation*, (Louisville: John Knox, 1989), 14.
3. J. Stevenson, ed., *A New Eusebius* (London: SPCK, 1957), 21.
4. Tertullian, *Fathers of the Church*, vol. 10, trans. Rudolph Arbesmann (New York: The Catholic University of America Press, 1950), 125.
5. Eberhard Bethge, *Dietrich Bonhoeffer: A Life in Pictures* (Philadelphia: Fortress Press, 1986), 233.
6. Ana Carrigan, *Salvador Witness: The Life and Calling of Jean Donovan* (New York: Simon and Schuster, 1984), 121.
7. James Brockman, *Romero: A Life* (Maryknoll: Orbis Books, 1989), 234, 248.
8. See the biography by Ana Carrigan, *Salvador Witness*. _Jean Donovan_
9. Jürgen Moltmann, *The Way of Jesus Christ: Christology in Messianic Dimensions*, trans. Margaret Kohl (Minneapolis, Minn.: Fortress Press, 1993), 156.
10. Quoted by James Cone in *Martyrdom Today*, ed. Johannes-Baptist Metz and Edward Schillebeeckx (New York: The Seabury Press, 1983), 76.
11. *A Testament of Hope*, 286.
12. Reinhold Niebuhr, *The Irony of American History* (New York: Charles Scribner's Sons, 1952), 163.
13. Quoted in Garry Wills, *Under God: Religion and American Politics* (New York: Simon and Schuster, 1990), 205.
14. Stephen B. Oates, *With Malice toward None: The Life of Abraham Lincoln* (New York: Mentor, 1978), 446.
15. Jürgen Moltmann, *The Crucified God* (Minneapolis, Minn.: Fortress Press, 1993), 278.
16. Henri J. M. Nouwen, *Our Greatest Gift* (San Francisco: HarperSanFrancisco, 1995), 67.
17. Augustine, *The City of God*, trans. Henry Bettenson (New York: Penguin Books, 1972), 1091.

CONCLUSION

1. Bodo, *The Way of St. Francis*, 105.
2. Walter Lowrie, *A Short Life of Kierkegaard* (Princeton, N.J.: Princeton University Press, 1970), 235–37.
3. Romano Guardini, *The Saints in Daily Christian Life* (Philadelphia: Chilton Books, 1966), 46–47.
4. Quoted by Foster, *Streams of Living Water*, 192.
5. Day, *The Long Loneliness*, 286.
6. Mother Teresa, *My Life for the Poor*, 1.